The Basics of Starting a Business Copy

Proper Planning Prevents P!ss Poor Performance

Julian Tansley

Journey Together LTD

Contents

Introduction

Life in the rat race can be pretty dull. In fact, it can often be infuriating. All you're doing is making someone else rich.

You get up every morning, drag yourself out of your warm, comfortable bed, and commute your way through nightmare traffic to the office. From there, you fill yourself up on an IV drip of coffee in an attempt to stay awake through the morning, willing the clock to move and land at 5 pm. During that time, you must endure people you dislike and bite your tongue a little too much for comfort. You go home exhausted.

Or maybe you don't want to be a part of this world; after all, there's much more to life, right? Perhaps you were made redundant and now realize there is no such thing as a secure job. Or maybe your children are grown up, and you finally have the time to pursue some of your own dreams. You might be a stay-at-home mom and would like a side income while taking care of your children.

Does any of that sound familiar?

We all need to get paid, but slaving away in a job that you don't enjoy or feel stuck in isn't going to bring you a whole lot of fulfillment. Living for the weekends means you're pausing your life most of the time, and there's only so much you can do in two days out of seven.

The truth is that life is far too short to sit and wonder if there's a better way, no matter what your situation. And that's one of the biggest reasons why people want to start a business of their own.

Freedom. Independence. Fulfillment. These are all things that having your own business brings to you.

Whatever your reason for choosing this book, the underlying will be obvious: you want to start a business and be your own boss. And why not? Lots of people do it, so why not you? You can be the one in the fancy office chair with a look of accomplishment on your face.

But starting a business isn't as simple as clicking your fingers and expecting everything to fall into place. Quite the opposite. Should you let that stop you?

Hell no!

Let's rewind a little. Firstly, welcome. You've come to the right place if you want to learn how to start a business and get the absolute truth. Consider me your fairy godfather of all things business, minus the tutu.

I won't sit here and tell you that everything will be easy and will all be a success. You don't need someone sugar-coating something that's not so simple. But I'm not going to tell you that it's impossible either. I will just give you the facts; from there, you can move forward and do whatever you need to.

Sounds good, right?

However, it's possible that you've tried to read up on starting a project like this before and tied yourself up in knots with the mountain of information out there. In all honesty, many books on starting a business give you the facts, but they do it in a way that's super-hard to follow for someone just starting out. They can be pretty boring too, don't you think?

Look, I get it; I've been there. You don't have to worry about any of that here. Instead, let's move through the subject together; picture us sitting with a coffee in hand, having a chat. Feel free to make yourself comfortable, I don't mind if you put your feet on the table.

***

What is Your 'Why'?

Before we get into any of the details, there's something you need to figure out first, and you're going to have to work this out on your own. What is your reason for wanting to start a business? What drives you? What pushes you toward this idea?

Most entrepreneurs have an underlying reason for wanting to start a business. Maybe it's because you're so sick of the corporate race, and you can't stand fake smiling every single day. Maybe you don't want to be a number in the system anymore and just going to work for a paycheck isn't enough. Perhaps you've come up with a brilliant idea but don't know where to start.

These are all great reasons for starting a business and fantastic motivators. Maybe yours isn't on that list, and that's fine. What you need to do before we get into the nitty-gritty of the subject is work out what is pushing you toward this avenue. Then, if things get rough (and at some point, they will), you can remember your 'why' and keep going.

Now, it's possible that you know you want to do this at this very moment in time, but you're not sure why. Don't panic! The coming chapters will help you unpick your motivations for choosing this book and then you can start to get things clear in your mind.

The truth is that there are a lot of pros and cons to starting a business. You'll have to ask yourself some tough questions and be brave enough to take small risks if you'll have the balls to overcome the hardships and get things moving. But once you start seeing the rewards slowly trickling in, the motivation will indeed arrive.

Let's Make Things Clear

I've been where you are now, so I know what you're thinking and the constant questions rolling through your mind. You're wondering if you're about to make a massive mistake, right? Well, maybe you will, but at least you'll know.

Starting a business needs plenty of clarity and careful moves, but the information is out there if you know where to look. Breaking that down into easy-to-digest pieces is my aim, and that's what I will do for you. It doesn't need to be quite so difficult or terrifying. This is an adventure!

By the end of this book, I hope you'll have a clear plan of what you need to do next, and the fire in your belly will be roaring hot.

So, grab a coffee, put your feet up, and let's get started!

Chapter One

Passion & Purpose: What's That All About?

What is the point of doing something if you don't have the first clue why you're doing it? Why should you do something if you really can't stand it?

For instance, you meet your friend for coffee to have a good time. You go to work because you want to get paid. You read a book to know what happens in the end. You watch a soccer match because you want your team to win.

Knowing your reason for doing something makes you do it. Otherwise, you're just wandering around without the first clue, lost in words.

Not a good look, in all honesty.

Before you even think about starting your business and making a move, you need to identify your passion and, to a certain degree, your purpose. That's what we're going to explore in this chapter. By the end, you should not only understand what this is all about, but you should be on your way to thinking about your own reasons for even starting a business.

***

Playing With the Fires of Passion

Having a passion for something means you're emotionally invested in it. You want to make it a success because it means something to you; in fact, it means the world to you. It's a hunger, a belief, and a genuine desire to do something and enjoy it. You care because it matters to you on a deeper level. It almost becomes your baby of sorts.

So that's why you can't just pick a business idea out of thin air and decide that you're going to go ahead with it. At some point, you'll stand in a daze and wonder why you bothered. Then, you'll just give up.

If you're passionate about your business, you'll be excited to make a success of it. You'll push yourself to come up with new ideas and solutions to niggling problems. You'll keep developing your vision and taking it further to keep it growing and evolving. It will become your dynasty, your legacy.

If you don't have a passion, you'll shrug your shoulders and return to watching whatever movie grabs your attention. It won't be all that important to you; if it goes wrong, you won't care. In fact, it will come as a relief to you because it was taking up too much of your time that you wish could be spent elsewhere.

The other side of the coin is that you shouldn't waste your time doing something that you don't find all that enjoyable. Life isn't supposed to be a slog; it's something we enjoy and fill with good things. While it's true that work is never 100% thrilling all the time, it should be something you embrace and enjoy for the most part.

Life is far too short to do something you can't stand. Where's the fun in that? In the middle of paying bills, making decisions, and doing all the other adult things, we forget that life is, in the end, supposed to be something we enjoy!

So, what is your passion?

What are you genuinely excited about? What makes you jump out of bed in the morning? Well, perhaps not jump, but at least get out of bed in the first place. Let's not get ahead of ourselves here.

Your passion can be something you're already doing, but maybe you've found yourself stuck with no new direction. Perhaps you have some skills but can't explore them in your current career. Maybe it's a hobby you love, and you could turn it into a money-making business idea. It doesn't matter what it is, but it does matter that you believe in it. At this point, it also doesn't matter what anyone else thinks about it.

I've heard so many people come up with an idea, get truly excited about it, and then push it to one side because some random nay-sayer they don't care about decides to laugh in their face or tell them it won't work. Do you know what these people are? Jealous. They're green in the face, totally Grinch-like. They wish they could come up with something that makes them so excited and joyful.

Ignore these people. They'll suck the life right out of you if you let them.

Of course, that doesn't mean that your close circle shouldn't support you because you'll need them. But we'll talk more about that later on.

Think about Mark Zuckerberg for a second. Whether you like Facebook or not, you must admit that the guy did good. He had an idea to help people chat over the miles and threw himself into it. His passion pushed him through people telling him it wouldn't work, and look at him now; the guy's loaded and owns one of the biggest businesses in the world.

Not bad for a nerdy kid, right?

When Passion Goes AWOL

It's entirely possible that you had a passion at some point, but you lost it along the way. Life happens sometimes. Maybe you became unhappy at work due to a poor manager or a falling out with a colleague, and everything became so toxic that you started just going to work, doing the basics, and going home. You became a work zombie.

It happens far more commonly than you might think.

When this happens, you need to send out an SOS to your passion and register it as a missing person. If something used to fill you full of joy and excitement, but it's disappeared, you need to take some time to work out why. That means going on your own personal journey of enlightenment.

How very Oprah, right?

But there's a lot of use in working out why something no longer fills you with the joy it used to. Maybe you just grew out of it, and that's fine. But if you lost your passion because of outside influences, it's time to reclaim what is yours.

Spend some time exploring what happened and whether you feel like you lost an opportunity along the way. It's never too late to take it back.

I know you're keen to get things moving and start your business journey, but I can't emphasize enough the importance of knowing your passion before you do. Take some time to discover or rediscover what makes your blood burn and bubble in the best way possible.

How will you know when you've found it? You'll feel it. Suddenly you'll feel excited, and your mind will start coming up with ideas almost without thinking. Some ideas might be terrible, but your passion has been lit, and the only way is up.

So, What About Purpose?

If you've ever read a self-help book or watched an advice show, you'll undoubtedly have heard the word 'purpose.' These days, we're all supposed to discover our purpose and walk around like we have it all figured out, as though it comes with a badge or a secret club membership.

The truth is that most of us haven't got the first clue what our purpose is.

Now, a purpose isn't a definite necessity for starting a business, but it can help you to feel more excited along the way. It will push you to keep going because you feel like you're on the right path.

So, what is purpose?

Well, it's not something you wake up knowing about one morning and suddenly feel enlightened. This isn't an episode of the Ricky Lake show. Instead, it's a sense of understanding that what you're doing is right for you. It's a reason something exists; in this case, it's the reason your business idea exists. It's something you can do for yourself or others that fill you with a sense of worth and fulfillment.

Understandably, purpose is a lot harder to find than passion, but they tend to co-exist. If you have passion, you've likely found your purpose, or at least on your way toward it.

Your purpose can also be your future goal. For example, once you start your business and make a profit regularly, you might set a goal to donate money to a charity close to your heart.

There is no 'one size fits all' type of purpose. Still, a few examples to give you a better idea:

- Exploring different cultures as you travel around the world
- Doing what you can to support your local community
- Choosing a social cause and raising awareness, e.g., food poverty or climate change

- Supporting your friends and family and always being positive
- Creating a business that is going to make a real difference to people's lives

The vital thing to remember is that your purpose might take a lot more time to figure out, so if it doesn't come to you very quickly, don't worry. There's nothing wrong with you. Maybe a sense of purpose will appear halfway along your business journey, and suddenly it will be like someone switched on a lightbulb. It's different for everyone.

Yet, if you're lucky enough to know your purpose from the start, there's no denying that it can help you stick on the right path and navigate the road bumps that might come your way. And sorry to break it to you, but it will get at least a bit bumpy at some stage.

It's Time for Homework

Wait, homework?

You didn't think you were signing up for out-of-hours work, did you?! Well, sorry to break it to you, but starting a business isn't just about making a decision and going for it. You need to plan the whole thing carefully.

I want you to understand what you're doing, why you're doing it, and what you need to do next. That means soul-searching and careful thinking.

In this chapter, we've talked about knowing your why, identifying your passion, and understanding the idea of purpose. You know why it's all vital now, but do you know your answers to the above?

That's your homework; don't expect to finish it in an hour.

So, let's focus on your passion for now, as it's far easier to work out than your purpose. Take some time to explore and answer these questions one by one:

- What do you find relaxing?
- What did you enjoy in your childhood and teenage years that you no longer do?
- Why did you stop doing those things?
- What subject can you talk about endlessly without getting bored?
- If you could do anything and money wasn't an issue, what would you do?
- What things do you find important in life?
- What things give you a sense of fulfillment?
- What things do you find stressful? What things drain your energy?
- Picture your ideal life in 5 years and 10 years. What does it look like? What are you doing?

- What makes you forget to eat and go pee?
- What do you want to be remembered for after you're gone?

Don't rush through these questions. Take each one in turn and write it down. Then, brainstorm your ideas. You don't have to write full sentences; I won't come around and check your work with a red pen. This is to prompt your mind into thinking about the answers to deep questions.

By asking these questions and pondering the answers, you'll start taking giant leaps toward discovering your true passion. After all, doing something you're passionate about makes work easier, more enjoyable, and in the end, more successful.

Chapter Two

Mindset is Key: Overcoming Fear & Self-Doubt

Starting a business is tricky... well, business. Unless you're bulletproof, you'll have moments of doubt, and there will likely be times when you wonder why you bothered in the first place. Like, is it meant to be this hard?

Sorry to break it to you, but in some ways, yes, it is. Because otherwise, wouldn't the success be pretty underwhelming?

But look at it like this – Bill Gates felt that way. Richard Branson felt that way. Oprah Winfrey felt that way. It's normal. So, when you start to panic and you're overwhelmed with 'what if' thoughts, ask yourself this: what would Oprah do?

In all seriousness, mindset is one of the most important things about starting a business. It's easy to place all your focus on things like capital, business plans, and marketing, and yes, they're essential, but laying the proper foundation is critical. Without it, you'll find yourself quickly slipping down a slide, leading to disappointment.

The business founder's mindset is something that few people consider. After all, you expect things to go wonderfully well or fail from the start. You don't think for a second that you're about to go on a journey asking you to jump over more hurdles than Karsten Warholm. He's a world champion hurdler, in case you didn't know.

But the hurdles are what make you stronger. Without those slight moments of doubt, the whole thing would be pretty dull, right? While you don't want a terrifying journey of constant issues, you don't want an ultra-smooth one either; that won't teach you anything, and you'll take everything for granted. Pitfalls and problems help us stop, think, reorganize, and find a different route. And none of that is terrible.

I know, I know, you want me to sit here and say if you do x, y, and z, then you'll succeed with flying colors. Maybe you will, but I won't lie to you either. Starting a business is hard, but with the right mindset, you'll be able to overcome whatever life decides to throw your way.

Wait, What is The Right Mindset?

So, what exactly do I mean about the right mindset?

A few pointers include:

- Knowing the importance of home and work-life balance

from the start

- Being a little emotionally detached from the whole thing
- Overcoming the employee mindset
- Dealing with stress – lots and lots of stress
- Why it's no good to be overwhelmed
- The importance of having a support system

Let's take a look at each one in turn, but before we do, there's one significant thing to remember – 'what if' won't help you.

Please, for everything good in this world, forget those two words.

I mentioned them earlier, but that was simply to illustrate a point. These two words will mess with your mind. What if you fail? What if you succeed? What if you pour all your life's savings into your business idea and it all blows up in your face? What if you end up rich?

Can you see what I'm getting at here? There's always a positive for every negative, so what's the point in wondering? Unless you have a crystal ball, and if you do, please share it, then wondering about the future isn't going to do you any good.

All you can do is lay the foundations, follow advice, listen to your gut, be sensible, and in some ways, hope for the best. Doing everything you can will avoid the worst-case 'what if' anyway. You don't need crystal balls or mystical tarot card readings for that.

You'll also spend all your time worrying about what might happen and taking your eye off the ball. You need all your decision-making wits about you here. Otherwise, you'll be too distracted to think clearly.

The Importance of Home & Work-Life Balance

The first element of the right mindset is about balance. It's normal to want to throw all your time and focus into your business; after all, it's your new baby, but it's a mistake. There has to be a line.

Balancing your home and working lives takes time and practice; there will likely be a few issues, but you'll learn to overcome them. Your relationships will suffer if you pour all your time and effort into your business. Your health will suffer. Similarly, if you throw all your time and effort into your home life, there's no point in trying to start a business.

There has to be a weighing-up and balancing process here.

So, how can you do that?

Give yourself set working hours that you dedicate to business matters. Once the clock strikes five, or whatever time you've set, you turn your working mind off and flick it back to social times. It won't come easily at first but persevere.

You might also find that keeping a notebook and pen handy or a notes app on your phone helps. Then, whenever you think of something outside of 'working hours,' you can jot it down, and you won't forget.

Also, the moment you think about canceling a meet-up with a friend or a date night for a business matter, give yourself a virtual slap and change your mind. We're talking metaphorically here; don't actually slap yourself.

The point is there must be a line between the two parts of your life because something will suffer when one starts to encroach on the other.

Staying Emotionally Detached

This one is super-hard. You're about to pour money, time, and effort into your idea, and of course, it will consume you, but it's VITAL that you remain a little detached. Being too emotionally involved in your business idea means you can't make solid, fact-driven decisions.

Going with your heart over your head might work in some situations, but it's rarely advisable when it comes to business.

I know what you're going to say: how can you stay emotionally detached from something you're passionate about? Well, there is that. But there must be a slight distance between you and the idea itself. Tell yourself that this may be something you're passionate about, but it's not the 'be-all and end-all.'

You will not be a strong leader or business owner if you're constantly becoming emotionally invested in every decision you must make. Visualize yourself standing back. Whenever a decision needs to be made, literally visualize a distance between the choice and you; in fact, imagine a forcefield that stops you from standing too close.

Learn to look at all the options and do not always go with whatever your gut tells you. Yes, sometimes your gut is right, but we're not talking about what color sweater you should wear that day or where you should go on vacation; we're talking about crucial fact-driven business decisions that need to be made carefully. By keeping an emotional distance between you and your business, you can serve it much better.

Being emotionally detached also means you don't become too stuck on one approach. For instance, maybe you start selling physical products, and it's not working out. If you're too attached to the idea, you won't give in; you'll keep pushing and pushing, even when nothing changes. However, when you have the ability to take a step back, you will simply throw that idea away, come up with a new one, and go again.

Also, I don't want to say this ... but in the unlikely (yet unfortunately possible) event that your business doesn't work out or you need to go back to basics once more, being detached will stop the whole thing from devastating your confidence. Then, you can reassess and build again. If you're too emotionally invested, the whole thing will destroy you.

Overcoming The Employee Mindset

If you've always worked for someone else, you'll undoubtedly have an employee mindset. You might not even realize that you do, but it's time to turn that mindset off and dedicate yourself to your new business owner's mindset.

You're not working for someone else now. You're working for yourself. You have no one to answer to but yourself and you have to make the decisions. That means being methodical and exploring all options. It also means no longer having to follow someone else's rules anymore; you're the boss! You can steer this ship in any direction you choose.

A big part of an employee mindset is that you rely upon someone else. You feel that your manager is the person who has to give you opportunities to grow and develop. But when you step outside of that, you realize that you have the power to do everything yourself. It's quite a feeling once you get into it.

You cannot wait for someone to tell you what to do anymore; you must put the wheels in motion and start making decisions for yourself. Doors will open when you do this; you don't need to wait for someone else to open them and ask you to walk through them.

It's time to start feeling a little more comfortable with being uncomfortable. And yes, I know that's somewhat of a contradiction, but a business owner has to live life on the edge to a degree. Not too close to the edge, of course. You don't want to fall off, but you need to learn how to teeter and balance without ending up with a broken leg or something else.

Dealing With Stress

Oh, there will be stress. There will be lots of stress.

First up, you need to make peace with this fact, but that doesn't mean you should allow it to consume you. Business owners face stress most days, but the key is knowing stress management techniques to avoid becoming chronically stressed because that's not good for you or your health.

A little earlier, I mentioned home and work-life balance. Well, that's a big step toward avoiding stress build-up. When you can close the door on your work life and relax with your loved ones, you're already doing a lot to manage stress. But what else can you do?

- **Make sure you get plenty of sleep.** That means going to bed at a reasonable time every night and waking up at the same time every day - give or take ten minutes or so.
- **Exercise regularly.** Those feel-good endorphins will ward off stress, clear your mind, and help you make more decisive decisions.
- **Talk about things.** If something bothers you, find someone you can trust and talk it over. You'll find the issue feels far less bothersome afterward.
- **Try meditation.** Yes, really. Meditation is fantastic for reducing stress and helping you to stay in the moment. In fact, mindfulness meditation is the best route for this. That way, you'll avoid panicking about the past or worrying about the future; you'll stay in the here and now, enjoying it and making better choices.
- **Have a day off.** As part of your new home and work-life balance approach, you also need at least one day off per week to destress and switch off your mind. The human brain might be pretty sophisticated, but it can only take on so much information at any one time; it needs a break!
- **Use time management techniques.** Finally, you'll feel much less stressed if you're in control of your workload. That means learning to manage your time and not letting everything mount up; remember, procrastination is the devil. Prioritize your to-do list daily, try the Pomodoro Technique, or Eat The Frog (not literally), and you'll find that

you cover all bases and won't miss anything important.

One of the biggest stressors for new business owners is the potential for losing money. Before, you probably had a regular salary coming in and all your bills covered. Now you're out there on your own, and it can be a little scary.

The thing is, it's like that for every business owner at the start. All you can do is plan and make solid choices, and once you start to see a profit, be sensible. Put some money away as a 'just in case,' and then keep going.

It's easy to doubt yourself and stay in a so-called safe situation because you avoid the anxiety of doing something different. But if you don't try, you'll never know. Think of the worst-case scenario here; if it goes wrong (and I'm not saying it will), you just rethink and go again.

Why It's No Good to Be Overwhelmed

Analysis paralysis is the fast track to feeling overwhelmed, and when that happens, burnout isn't too far away. You really can't run a business when you're burnt out.

Analysis paralysis means you can't make a decision because you've sat there and overthought it to the point where it's a mountain in your mind. You're paralyzed, stuck, and don't have the first clue what to do.

You see, you can overthink, and you can prepare too much too. That doesn't mean you should jump to the first idea that pops into your mind and go with it, but you shouldn't meditate over it to obsessive levels, either. It's about finding a middle ground.

When you're overwhelmed, you'll put everything off until another day because you don't know what to do first. It's almost like your feet are stuck in quicksand, and you can't move. Not only is it frustrating, but the chances of you making the wrong move are pretty high.

The thing is, when you care about something, you always want to make the right choices, and that's commendable but isn't going to help you very much. Avoiding analysis paralysis comes down to learning to trust yourself. You can never make a 100% right decision without any risk, there will always be an element of doubt, and there will always be other things at play that you can never totally predict. But you can make the best choice with the information you have and then leave the rest down to good fortune.

I know that sounds like flimsy advice, but you cannot control every single thing around you. And if you attempt to, you'll feel overwhelmed and stressed that you'd do more harm than good.

When you have a decision to make, sit down and create a shortlist of choices/solutions. Then write down the pros and cons of each one. Go with the one with the least cons and the most pros. Never attempt to find an answer with zero cons because it doesn't exist.

The Importance of Having a Support System

You can't do this alone. You might think you can be all heroic and prove everyone wrong, but you're only human. At some point, you will need to talk something over with someone or simply scream at the ceiling and have someone nod along to your random outbursts.

Having a support system will make your life as a business owner much easier and more enjoyable. A little earlier, I talked about not listening to people who tell you that your business idea isn't going to work. These aren't the types of people I'm referring to here. I'm talking about close friends, family members, a partner, your business partner, or like-minded people who are keen to get out there and do something with their lives too.

You don't have to explain every move you're making with your business, but having a support system means that when you're struggling a little or just need some advice from someone with an outside view, you've got someone to go to.

It's pretty invaluable.

***

The Right Mindset Reduces Fear & Self-Doubt

Having your brain in the right place means you can overcome anything life throws at you. But don't expect to never feel a tiny twinge of doubt or to be scared about things. It will happen at some point because that's part of life.

It isn't about cutting out doubt and fear entirely. It's about reducing it to the point where you can accept it as a regular part of the business deal and move past it. That's what getting into the right mindset can help you with.

It also means moving slowly.

Don't assume that you need to hit the ground running and zoom around like a Formula One driver. Slow and steady wins the race here. While you'll no doubt want to get things moving and past this uncertain, uncomfortable part, you don't want to rush and miss something important.

Take your time. This isn't a race.

***

Ready For Some More Homework?

Yes, this is going to be a regular thing. Sorry to break it to you!

Developing the right mindset for the job isn't going to happen overnight, but you can encourage things by preparing in advance. An excellent place to start is with a plan to ensure you keep that home and work-life balance intact.

So, your homework for this chapter is to plan out your day. I'm not suggesting you become a robot and follow the same routine every day, but what time are you going to get up in the morning? What are your working hours going to be? At what time will you stop work and focus all your attention on family/friends/partner/children, and basically just chill a little? What time are you going to stop for lunch? What day are you going to have off from work every week?

Having a working structure is so important, and while routine might sound boring, it will save you from going too far in either direction and ending up burnt out. You're not going to be that person that sits in the office burning the midnight oil.

Chapter Three

Help! I'm All Out of Ideas!

Your brain has suddenly emptied itself of all useful ideas. You know you want to do something, but you can't quite put your finger on what. Maybe you know what you don't want to do, but that's where your brain energy ends.

Don't worry, it's a pretty common situation. It's a little like when you have to decide what to make for dinner, but you suddenly can't remember the names of any dishes you regularly make. Decision pressure.

Not everyone who decides they want to start a business knows exactly what they're going to do. Maybe you know the industry type you want to enter, but the groundbreaking idea evades you. It doesn't mean that you're not ready. It just means you need to do some research and see if any suggested ideas grab your attention.

In this chapter, I will help get those creative juices flowing. I will talk you through 20 business ideas, including the pros and cons of each one. Maybe you'll see an idea in this list and be like, "Yes! That's the one," or perhaps it sparks a different idea in your mind.

Either way, it will help you to see the types of things you can do and how every idea has its pluses and minuses.

***

What Do You Want from Your Business?

Before settling on an idea, it's important to know what you want from your business and what you don't. Of course you want to make money. That's a given. But what else?

Ponder these questions for a moment:

- Do you want to work with a team of people so you have a sociable vibe every day?
- Would you instead work in a small team?
- Do you want to make a difference in some specific niche?
- Do you want to make just enough money to cover your current salary, or do you want to go all out and make more?
- How many hours do you want to work per day?
- What do you want your business to look like 5 years from now?
- What about 10 years from now?
- Do you want to be involved in every business decision and transaction, or are you happy to delegate?

- Do you want to provide goods or services?
- What type of people do you want to sell to/help?

When you can picture how you want your business to be, it's easier to settle on an idea. It's just as important to know what you don't want because when you know that, you can avoid heading in that direction at all costs.

For instance, if you don't want to work more than 4 hours per day, you'll need to choose an idea that allows for passive income to a certain degree. Otherwise, you could choose the wrong idea and find that you must put in the hard graft of more than 6 hours per day. When your business starts to go in a direction that doesn't please you, your passion will dampen, and you're more likely to give up.

Remember, this is your business and your story. You can shape it and tweak it how you see fit.

20 Inspiring Business Ideas

Let's assume you don't have the first clue what you want to do. Or you have a tiny idea but are open to suggestions. You've come to the right place.

Let's get started!

Online Reselling

Online reselling means that you source items, such as clothing or accessories, and then sell them for a profit. This is, as the name suggests, all done online. As such, you can sit in your pajamas and run your business from your sofa.

You can find clothing items in your own closet, in your friends' closets, in charity stores, thrift markets, garage sales, eBay, literally anywhere. And once you find good-quality items, you decide how much you're going to sell them for, list them, and wait for the cash to roll in. You can start using sites like eBay or Poshmark and then open your own reselling website once you become more established.

Pros:

- You can quickly start this type of business as a side hustle and then branch out once you're confident you're making a good, regular profit.
- You can branch out into different items. For instance, you can start with clothes and then branch out into accessories or even homewares.
- Setting up a website to sell your items on is easy.
- Working online means you can work from home and avoid commuting.

Cons:

- Sourcing items takes time, especially for quality items.
- You'll need to spend on your items before you can sell

them.

- People are more likely to spend on well-known brands, which cost money from the get-go.
- You'll need to post items out to buyers.
- You'll probably work alone initially and might not like that idea.

Cleaning Services

Do you love cleaning? Enjoy spending your days in rubber gloves? If so, you can make some cold, hard cash from your love of scrubbing!

Established cleaning businesses are in high demand, thanks to the busy lives that most people lead these days. You can start off doing the cleaning yourself, but over time, as your business grows, you can delegate tasks out to members of staff, if you choose to hire.

Most cleaning services offer their services to homes, offices, schools, event auditoriums, etc., and charge by the hour.

Pros:

- You only need transportation and cleaning supplies to get started - very few overheads.
- You can easily promote your cleaning business online for very little cash.
- You can branch out by employing cleaners as your business grows.

- You don't need specific qualifications, you just need to be good at what you do!

Cons:

- You'll need to offer additional services to stand out from other cleaning businesses - there are many out there! These services could include waxing floors, steam-cleaning, power-washing, etc.

- Building up your business will rely upon word-of-mouth marketing to a certain degree, which could mean slow business growth.

- One poor-quality job could cost you further contracts - high quality is key!

Online Teaching

You'll have to get dressed for this one, but nobody will know you're wearing your pajama bottoms if you wear a smart shirt on top! Online teaching is a great way to work from home and earn cash, teaching people about something you have a skill in. For example, can you play a musical instrument very well? Can you teach English or another language?

Teaching English as a foreign language to online foreign students is a very in-demand service, and this can be taught to both children and adults. All you will need is a TEFL certificate, which can be obtained relatively easily through distance learning. However, if you don't want to teach English, you can teach any subject you're skilled in.

Pros:

- Make the most of your talent and make money from it.
- You can choose your own working hours.
- You will charge a flat hourly rate and offer a set number of lessons for a bundle price.
- Relatively easy to fit around your regular home life.

Cons:

- You'll need to build up your reputation as a tutor before large numbers of students come your way.
- If you want to teach a language, you'll need a qualification to back up your skills.
- Lots of competition out there.

Pet-Sitting

Establishing a pet-sitting business could be an excellent option for you, especially if you're a big fan of furry friends. If you're not keen on animals, you'll probably want to skip this one!

A considerable number of people have pets, and not everyone wants to take their animal away with them when they head off for a business trip or on vacation. That's where you come in. You establish a service to look after their pets in their absence, in their own home. This benefits your customers because most people don't like the idea of taking their pets to another place while they're away.

Pros:

- If you love animals, this is a great business idea.
- You can run more than one business while doing this; you'll be sitting in your customer's home, so you can work online doing something else simultaneously.
- You'll save on household bills while you're pet-sitting.
- No overheads.

Cons:

- If you're not a dog or cat lover, avoid it.
- You might not like the idea of staying in someone else's home.
- Building up a business such as this will require you to have some experience and happy customers to put your new customers' minds at rest. They won't let anyone stay in their home and look after their pet!

Bookkeeping Services

If you have an eye for numbers and experience with bookkeeping and accounting, you could establish a bookkeeping business, either online or in person. You could also offer both options, allowing you to branch out to more customers.

You can start with one client and build up from there, but you must not take on too much, as one bookkeeping mistake could ruin your reputation!

Pros:

- You can offer either an in-person or online service. Helping you reach more people.
- Modern technology makes bookkeeping an accessible online business option.
- You can set your own working hours.
- You can set an hourly rate or charge a retainer over a long-term contract.

Cons:

- You'll need to purchase bookkeeping software to allow clients to access their records at the same time as you.
- You will need to have a qualification to encourage trust.
- Quite a challenging business idea to get off the ground - but not impossible!

Consulting

Do you have a lot of knowledge of a particular subject that you can pass on to other people? This isn't the same as online teaching, although it does sound similar. The difference with consulting is that you act as an adviser rather than a teacher.

For instance, if you're a whiz at SEO, you could offer your consulting services to businesses who want to improve their own Search Engine Optimization. But it doesn't stop there; there are countless subjects you can look at, such as marketing, leadership, communication, etc.). As your business grows, you can recruit consultants to branch out and help more clients.

Pros:

- You can share your expertise with those who need it, giving you a sense of fulfillment.
- This type of job is collaborative, so you'll meet many people from different walks of life.
- Consultants can often charge high hourly rates once established.
- You can work as a consultant either online or in person.

Cons:

- Consulting is a tricky business to get off the ground. You'll need to be patient! After all, it will take a good amount of time to build a reputation.
- Finding high-quality consultants to work alongside you may be difficult.
- You will also need to pay your consultants a good wage, so wait until you're well-established before hiring.

A Physical Shop

One of the most common business ideas is to open a brick-and-mortar shop and sell actual goods and services. You can sell anything you want, depending on what you like and the other competition in the area.

The plus point is that you will go to work and come home again; when you work online, finding that separation between home and work can be a little more difficult.

Pros:

- Having your own shop feels like a real accomplishment because it's something you can see and touch.
- You can become a part of the local community, getting to know your customers.
- It's also easier to give something back to the local community when you have a shop.

Cons:

- Finding a shop can be expensive and time-consuming.
- Marketing your store may be difficult and depends heavily on the competition in the local area.
- Taxes, rent, electricity, gas, staff, etc., can all cost a small fortune over the course of just one month.
- Managing stock can also be tricky as you don't want too much or too little.

Transcription Services

If you have a relatively fast typing speed, setting up a transcription business could be for you. In this situation, you will have clients who need spoken transcripts typed out into a specific format.

It's your job to get it all down onto paper correctly, quickly, and without mishearing something and making a blunder.

There are many different types of transcription, but medical transcription is in-demand.

Pros:

- A fast typist can often get a lot of transcription done in one day, which means a good amount of earned cash.
- Over time, you can employ other transcribers to build your business.
- You can advertise your services online to onboard more clients.
- You can work from home at first and then move into an office space if you want to.

Cons:

- A typing speed of at least 120 wpm is usually necessary.
- You'll need the necessary equipment, such as a foot pedal, earphones, and software.
- It's not always easy to decipher accents on recordings.

Freelance Writing & Proofreading

Setting up a freelancing writing and/or proofreading business means you can work as your own boss and take on clients to suit your needs. You can ghostwrite eBooks, blog posts, and articles and even proofread other writers' work.

Signing up for a freelancing website to find clients and slowly build your business from there is a good idea. This type of business is all about reputation, so don't expect to have several jobs all at once. However, over time, you may find this can be a lucrative business that you will enjoy if you have a passion for words.

Pros:

- If you love writing, you'll find this job is more of a pastime than a job and one that brings cash your way.
- You can choose the projects you take on, giving you control over your workload.
- You can manage your own time, giving you a better home and work-life balance.
- You can work from anywhere, as long as you have a laptop and Internet connection.

Cons:

- If you're ghostwriting, your name won't appear on any of your work.
- Not all clients are easy to work with!
- There is a lot of competition out there.
- You'll need to build up your business slowly over time; it won't be a fast process.

Laundromat

You'll be surprised at the sheer number of people who will happily send their laundry to a laundromat. It saves them time and, for those who are living in apartments that don't have individual washing machines, you'll be a lifesaver!

If you're one of those people who enjoy the smell of freshly washed clothes, a laundromat could be a good business idea for you. These are particularly successful in large cities, full of busy people.

Pros:

- There is always demand for laundromat services.
- You can expand your business in the future to include ironing, dry cleaning, etc.
- In some cases, you may be able to work from home until you start building your business, although this will depend on the amount of space you have.

Cons:

- There are likely other laundromats in your area, so you'll have to market your services well to beat the competition.
- You'll need to invest in machinery as your business grows, e.g., large washing machines, drying machines, etc.
- Laundromats are area specific, so it's not a business you can grow beyond your local area.

Home Care Services

Do you have a passion for helping others? If so, offering home care services could be gratifying and allow you to develop your own business model. Home care services can be for people with disabilities, the elderly, children in need, etc. In most cases, you'll need a social care and childcare qualification if you're working with children, but after that, you're free to register with the appropriate bodies and set up your business.

You can charge an hourly or daily rate and provide basic care for people in their own homes. This is an in-demand service these days as more and more people prefer to stay in their own homes for as long as possible and avoid expensive care homes.

Pros:

- A real sense of achievement from helping other people.
- An in-demand role that could lead to a lucrative business.
- You can hire other carers as your business grows.
- If you have transportation, you can travel to more homes.

Cons:

- You'll need some qualifications, and depending upon your country of origin, you'll probably need to register with a professional body.
- Travel may take up some of your time, therefore cutting down on your profits.
- Building up your business depends on reputation, which could take time.

Digital Marketing Services

The business world is moving online more and more as the years roll by, meaning businesses need to get out there and market their services. Competition is fierce, so if you're someone who knows the secrets to getting noticed while optimizing online reach, you'll be an in-demand service yourself.

Many businesses no longer want to pay for an entire marketing department and prefer outsourcing their marketing needs. That's where you come into play. Putting together a complete marketing plan and acting as a consultant can be a very lucrative endeavor.

Pros:

- An in-demand service with a lot of room for growth.
- You can branch out into affiliate marketing or influencing yourself.
- You can work from home.

Cons:

- Competition in the marketing sphere is extremely fierce, which means you'll need to fight to be noticed from the get-go.
- This is a cutthroat business; one small mistake can easily lose a client.
- You'll need to stay up to date with all the latest niche developments, as well as online marketing news.

Your Own Food Truck

If you love to cook but don't fancy the idea of opening your own restaurant, how about the freedom of a food truck instead? And no, this doesn't mean you have to flip burgers - although you can if you want to!

Food trucks are the latest trend, and we all know that street food is seriously in fashion. While you'll need to purchase a truck and modify it to make sure it fits in with all local regulations in terms of health and safety, you could be cooking and driving to your heart's content!

Pros:

- You can move around, therefore making the most of the local clientele.
- If you choose a food idea that isn't prevalent in your area, you'll probably be a big success.
- Far less stressful than a restaurant.
- Fewer overheads.

Cons:

- You'll have to buy the truck and modify it, which is a considerable start-up cost.
- You'll need to check local rules regarding where you can park and sell your food.
- You'll need to vigorously market your food truck, as people know less about trucks than restaurants.

Gardening Services

If you love the Great Outdoors and Mother Nature is your best friend, how about starting a gardening business? You could offer lawn care services, planting, weeding, etc. This is especially beneficial for people who simply don't have the time to care for their gardens - which is most people these days!

All you need is the necessary equipment, which, if you're a keen gardener, you'll probably already have, and transportation. Market your business online and in the local area, and you're good to go!

Pros:

- You'll be doing something you truly love.
- You can expand your services to meet seasonal needs.
- As your business grows, you can hire other gardeners, helpers/apprentices.
- Marketing a service like this in the local area isn't difficult.

Cons:

- If you don't already have the equipment, you'll need to purchase it before you start.
- You'll need transportation, e.g., a van.
- You may find this kind of work is quite seasonal, which may limit your income during the colder months.
- You may need a license, depending on your local area and the services you provide.

A Real Estate Business

There is a considerable amount of money in real estate, and if you enjoy helping people find their dream homes, this could be your ideal business.

Opening your own real estate agency means you'll need to register, and you'll probably need to complete a course. However, these aren't particularly lengthy. From there, you'll connect with landlords and property owners to sell/rent out their properties to eager clients. Each time you're successful, you'll earn a commission and probably a rate of pay from the landlord.

Pros:

- A very lucrative business once you're established.
- You can work with several landlords/property owners simultaneously, increasing your business reach.
- A fulfilling feeling once you match someone with their dream home.

Cons:

- It takes a while to become established, and competition is fierce.
- You must complete a course and register as an estate agent.
- You will need to hire staff once you start juggling a few different contracts, which adds to your overhead.
- You'll probably need an office, which means more overheads.

Personal Trainer

The health and wellness industry is booming, meaning people are spending their money on services such as personal trainers. Not everyone has the time to go to the gym; if they do, they want fast results. That's where you come in.

You will need to be a qualified personal trainer to start this kind of business. From there, you can work freelance, marketing your business in local gyms and online, usually through social media.

Pros:

- You'll gain real satisfaction in helping people reach their health goals.
- You can set your own hours.
- You can work with several clients simultaneously, increasing business growth and profits.
- You can work inside a gym (by arrangement) or outdoors. In time, you may be able to rent your own studio.

Cons:

- You'll need to be a qualified personal trainer. Depending upon local regulations, you may need to register with a professional body.
- Competition is fierce, and you'll need to market your business heavily.
- Managing clients' expectations can be demanding!

Dropshipping

Do you remember a little earlier, we talked about online reselling? Well, dropshipping is a little like that, but without the stock.

In effect, you set up your own eCommerce store and sell items to customers. But you don't have those items; you source them from a reputable retailer and sell them for a profit. The retailer will handle the sending of the items. You just pay the retailer and keep the spare for yourself.

It sounds too good to be true, right? Well, it's not easy, but if your dropshipping business is booming, you'll make a good amount of cash for little effort.

Pros:

- A lucrative business idea with little effort.
- You don't need to stock products, which saves space and means you can work from home.
- You can branch out into other items, expanding your business.
- You can have more than one dropshipping business at any one time.

Cons:

- You'll need to find reputable and high-quality retailers to work with, as they're dealing with your clients, and if they let you down, you get the heat.
- A lot of administrative work if you have to chase suppliers for items, e.g., if you receive an email from a buyer.

Sell Your Photography

Are you a keen photographer? Or do you have a natural talent for snapping at the right moment? If you have the equipment, why not profit from selling your photographs and setting up your business?

You could take as many photographs as possible and then upload them to stock photography sites. Then, when someone buys one of your images, you are paid directly.

Pros:

- If you love photography, you're making money from something you enjoy.
- You can do everything online, giving you plenty of downtime between photography sessions.
- You can branch out to photography services, such as weddings, etc.

Cons:

- It may take a while to build up a reputation.
- Selling images on stock sites alone may not result in huge revenue.
- Competition is likely to be fierce.

Childcare Services

For this one, you are going to need childcare qualifications. Otherwise, nobody in their right mind will let you look after their children! But if you are qualified or willing to get qualified and love children, why not start your own childcare business? There's a lot of paperwork to go through, and you'll need to register with the necessary bodies, but it could be an excellent way for you to enjoy what you do and earn cash at the same time. Of course, you also get the feel-good factor of helping out a family too.

Pros:

- Could be a fun business idea if you enjoy spending time with children.
- There will always be a demand for childcare, especially if you can make it affordable.
- You can offer out-of-hours services for extra cash, e.g., during the holidays or early evenings for parents who are working late.

Cons:

- There is a lot of competition out there.
- You'll need qualifications and must register, which is time-consuming and costly.
- Reputation is everything with childcare, so you'll need to build up your portfolio of experience.

Sewing/Alteration Specialist

Once upon a time, this was called a tailor or a seamstress, but we've moved on from those old names! If you're handy with a sewing machine and it's something you enjoy, you could set up an alterations service. You can do this from your own home or have your own studio, whatever works for you.

Pros:

- You can work from home at first or continue working from home even when established.
- If you already have a spare room and a sewing machine, you're good to go!
- You can branch out into other services, such as making clothes.

Cons:

- You'll need to work to strict deadlines.
- You'll need to promote your services quite heavily at first, e.g., using social media and the online world in general; word-of-mouth marketing will only get you so far.
- Carpal tunnel? Well, maybe not that, but sewing all day long could give you plenty of aches and pains in your wrists.

Do any of these ideas float your boat? If not, have they given you some other inspiration? The aim is to show you how diverse the whole starting a business deal can be. You don't have to go down the 'regular' route if you don't want to; this is your business, and you can do whatever you want with it!

The important thing is that you choose something you're going to enjoy. Remember, this business will take up a lot of your time, and life is far too short to spend it doing something you grow tired of quickly. After all, that's the whole reason you're looking to try something new in the first place, right?

***

Homework Time!

It's that time again!

This chapter has been an inspiring one, or hopefully so, anyway. The idea here is that you should think of new ideas and decide whether they're for you. But that doesn't mean you should have pinpointed one just yet.

Take your time with this. If you already know what you want to do, well, what are you waiting for? But if not, don't fret. The longer you take to decide, the more sure you'll be, and that's never a bad thing.

So, homework. Your homework for this chapter is to pull out the ideas from this chapter that you like and spend some time focusing on each one. Is it something you feel you might want to do? And if not, is there something connected to those ideas that get you thinking instead? Follow the same process for each shortlisted idea and see where you stand at the end of it.

Chapter Four

Googalize Opportunities, Competitors, & Demand

I've got some surprising news for you.

Coming up with an idea is just a tiny part of the puzzle. You might think you've overcome a massive hurdle by deciding what your business will be about/what it will do, but in reality, that's just a tiny step. There's still a long, long way to go.

Yes, I know that's not what you wanted to hear, but I'm telling you straight!

Once you've come up with an idea, you must test it out a little. And it's wise not to get too attached to it at this moment. You might do some research and then realize that it's not the best idea in the world after all. And that's okay! You'll settle on an idea when it feels right, and the research backs it up.

For now, keep your rough idea, or even ideas, close to you and do some research.

So, what's next? Well, you need to become an investigator. You need to work out if there is demand for your goods/services and who your competitors will be, and then try to figure out if there are current opportunities. If not, where can you wave a magic wand and try to find some?

Consider this stage as your beta stage. By the end, you'll be 100% sure of your idea, and your business should start to take shape in your mind. It's worth going through this process to feel that excitement level, right?

Does Anyone Want You?

That sounds harsh, doesn't it? Well, yes, but it's a question you need to ask. Not about you as a person, because, of course, someone wants you, but about your business idea.

What I'm trying to say is, is there a demand for your idea?

You can come up with an idea that you're crazy passionate about, but if nobody else is, you won't make any money. You need to find the middle ground between a product you want to sell, a service you want to provide, and something people want and need. Until you reach that point, don't set your heart on anything; remember, you need to keep a certain amount of emotional detachment here!

But after that point, you need to get your persuasion on and make them spend cash in your direction.

So, how can you find out if there is demand for your idea?

The only real way to find out is to do some market research. That way, you can determine whether there is a market for your product or service before you start pouring time and money into it. Skip this step, and you'll be in an epic pickle!

Working out whether anyone is going to want to have anything to do with your idea isn't as difficult as it may seem. Sure, you can assemble a detailed questionnaire and collate all the responses, but do you have time for that? And most people aren't interested in filling in surveys these days anyway.

Instead, there are faster ways to get an idea of whether you're in vogue or not.

- **Look at the competition** - We will spend some time on this subject shortly, so I won't go into too much detail. But, generally speaking, the more competition, the bigger the demand. If you do a quick search and you find many businesses selling the same things you want to sell or offering the same services, you know people like it. Of course, you need to come up with a twist on your offerings to convince people that they should choose you over everyone else, but overall, an indicator of demand is moderate to high competition.

- **Throw it into Google** - The more you Google something, the more information you find. If pages and pages of results come up, people are talking about it. If you see very little, well, nobody is interested. That doesn't mean they won't be; you could be the first to pioneer a new invention, but for your first business venture, it's best to avoid trying to be Alexander Graham Bell and stick to something people know about.

- **Scour social media** - Social media may be a pain in the ass at times, but you have to admit that it's got its plus points. If you want to reach out to a huge number of people in record time, social media is your friend. Search for groups related to your idea and see what comes up. Then, read the replies and gain information that way. People will talk about their problems and wants in these groups, and that's a real 'in' for you.

- **Interact in groups** - Sticking with social media for a moment; when you find groups related to your idea, join them, and interact with members. You don't have to jump in and tell them that you're going to start a new business. In fact, it's preferable that you don't, but you can ask searching questions and find the responses you're looking for. You could even be blatant and say something like, "I've always looked for ... (insert idea), but I haven't been able to find it, have you?" and you'll get responses about where it is (e.g., your competition), or how much demand there is. This is the modern-day version of surveys, and it's a million times faster and more accurate.

Once you know there is demand for your idea, you've taken one step toward making it a reality. If you find that there isn't enough demand, think again. It doesn't mean you can't move forward, but you may find it harder to get your business off the ground.

***

Networking Up a Storm

Once you've ascertained that there is some amount of demand for the product or service you're eyeing, it's time to connect with people who can help you in some way. And unfortunately, that means doing the one thing most people hate: networking.

Yes, networking means selling your idea and yourself to some degree, but it's a very beneficial process. The more people you speak to, the more your name is out there, and the more chance there is of finding someone who can push your new business idea to the next level.

A detailed Google search will help you identify people in your industry that hold some clout. I'm not talking about CEOs here, but knowledgeable people who regularly hold seminars and talks. These people are usually very open to helping wherever they can. Otherwise, they wouldn't hold seminars! So, find out when these conferences, seminars, and events are, and make sure you clear some space in your diary to attend.

It's a good idea to have some business cards put together so you can give them out when you attend these events. You never know who you will accidentally end up talking to; even a chance meeting on your way out of the bathroom could allow you to meet someone influential! Then, once you've chatted, you can give them your business card, allowing them to reach out to you after the event.

Everyone's an "Expert"

However, you need to be careful of taking too much notice of so-called experts on social media. We live in a world where everyone shares their opinions and advice online.

If you find something that grabs your attention, you should triple-check the facts. Digest what feels relevant and valuable. They might give you helpful tips and tricks. But avoid becoming too enamored with an influencer or other person who claims to know everything.

However, that doesn't mean the online world isn't useful because you don't always have to network in person to find interesting stuff. YouTube is an excellent source of information, and you'll no doubt find countless videos in whatever niche you're aiming toward.

You can also buy online courses to learn more but only do this once you're sure what you want to do. You don't want to waste money at this point, and these courses can be pretty expensive.

Who Are Your Competitors?

We know that if an idea is in demand, there will be competitors. But that doesn't mean you should throw yourself headfirst into an industry saturated with competition. What you should do is look for an area that has a moderate amount of competition. That way, you know there's demand for that product or service, but you know you're not losing before you even start.

For instance, you could decide that you're going to set up a nail bar in your local town. That's a great idea because lots of people enjoy having their nails done, but if there are already five nail bars in your town and they're not that far away from one another, what makes you different?

If you have a widely different idea from everyone else and you can offer prices that are very competitive, well, there's your 'in.' But if you offer the same service, people are far more likely to stick with what they know.

That's what your market research will tell you.

But once you have decided what area you want to enter, you need to identify your competition and do some digging. That information will help you determine how you can offer something slightly different, whether you can offer lower prices, and how you can market your services to make your business stand out above the rest.

You also have an advantage at this point because nobody knows who you are, which means your competitors don't know either. You can fly under the radar and find out all the information you need!

There are several things you need to find out about your main competitors:

- What are their strengths and weaknesses are
- What are their strategies, e.g., marketing

- Their price range
- How they have developed their products and services

Understanding their strengths and weaknesses helps you gain a competitive edge because you can make their weaknesses your strengths. So, if they're pretty weak at social media marketing, that's where you need to excel. If they don't tend to diversify their products and only stick with one model, you can make that your area of expertise.

Industry publications are one of the things to keep your eye on. These are specialized magazines and journals that often feature interviews or articles on successful businesses in that particular niche and any upcoming businesses currently making waves. You can also find many of these in online versions.

Explore their website carefully and look at their social media presence. What do they shout about the most? What do people say about them? What are their pricing points and policies?

The truth is, examining your competition was a lot harder several decades ago because people had to do all of this under the radar and on foot. You have Google, and Google is your best friend.

Opportunities Are Everywhere ... You Just Have to Find Them

You've got a lot of information by now, so now you need to start looking for opportunities to test your products and services. You're still a long way off launching them, but this stage will allow you to know what tweaks you need to make before you arrive at that point.

As part of your networking process, you can find partners or collaborators to help you create and market your products or services. This can be an excellent way to find new opportunities because those people have connections too. In essence, networking isn't just about finding information. It's getting your name out there and looking for small glimmers of opportunity that could, at some point in the future, turn into something massive. Never overlook an opportunity to talk with someone or give your business card - you never know!

Testing, Testing, 1,2, 3!

Of course, opportunities are a chance to test your product and find out what you need to tweak. When putting your product together, shop around to find the best quality at the best price. For instance, if you're going to make something to sell, make sure the materials you use are good quality but that they don't cost you the earth, to begin with. It's no good starting with a loss, but at the same time, it's no good starting with low-quality materials because people will smell a rat from the get-go.

It can be a difficult piece of middle ground to find, but it will set you up for the long run. Focus on quality, and the rest will fall into place; your customers aren't stupid. They will know if they're being sold rubbish!

You could also set up a stall at an event and use this to talk to people and give them free samples of your products or services.

Testing your ideas in the real world before launching them in the market is an important step. Your idea works in your head, but that doesn't mean you have it all ironed out in reality. If you spend some time finding opportunities to test things out beforehand, you'll save time and money in the not-too-distant future.

And while it might seem like a great idea to test your ideas and products on your friends and family members, remember that they're probably a little biased and aren't giving you the entire story in some cases. You need to go further than that and test your ideas on people who don't even know you; those are the people who will be as honest as can be. And remember, total honesty is what you need at this point!

Take on board every single comment you receive and address them one by one, even if they don't seem all that important at first. Even if someone makes a passing comment about the color of your product, pay it some attention. Maybe they're onto something.

By covering all bases during your testing phase, you'll find the rest of the process goes a whole lot smoother.

***

Yes, More Homework!

Talking, testing, and researching may seem like hard work, but it's the foundation on which you can build.

When you take the time to cover these bases, you'll find useful information to put into your development phase. That way, you know that you're moving toward something more likely to be a success.

It's easy to assume that competition makes life more challenging, but it's a good thing. Competition means there is demand for your idea, giving you something to work against. Your competitors will push you to be better. Otherwise, you may become complacent and tick along without going as far as you can.

By checking for demand before moving forward, you're keeping that emotional distance between you and your idea. There's no point in trying to do something which there's no demand for!

So, now you know the basics, what is your homework?

- Sit down and spend some time on your computer or phone. Identify your three biggest competitors. Make sure you're not trying to compete with someone like Apple or Amazon but with businesses that are on the same scale as you and who will serve the same audience.

- For each competitor, identify three strengths and three weaknesses.

- For each strength and weakness, how can you work against that? How can you use that information to stand out?

Chapter Five

A 'Number' of Things You Should Know

It's time to grab your calculator, as understanding the math behind your business idea are more Lego blocks you need to build your business.

Consider the financial side of things your house's foundation. You know you can't build a house without laying the foundations first because it'll just fall down like a series of dominoes? Well, your business is the same.

Don't worry if numbers aren't your thing - you don't need to be a mathematician to plan your business. But you need some rough figures down on paper so you'll know whether it's a go-er or you need to spend a little more time planning!

Keeping Your Wits About You

Before we delve into specifics, there's one thing I want to mention to you. The Internet can be a wonderful place, full of opportunities to learn and research. It's a true melting pot of advice for people trying to set up their first business.

In our last chapter, I talked about how Google is your best friend right now, and that's totally true. But the Internet also has some dark corners with some very questionable numbers. I feel like I am repeating myself but be aware of false advertising about 'get rich quick schemes.'

Following this chapter's steps, you'll understand the difference between revenue, profit, and your bottom line. You can use that information to set up your business and move through those tricky first few months or years.

Don't be Afraid of The Numbers

Starting a business is exciting but also scary in many ways. The financial side of things is where stuff gets real and often where people stumble because they rush this part, often through not understanding.

I advise you to take your time and reach out for help if you don't understand something. It's much better to take your time right now and work it out properly than to rush and realize that a few months down the line, you didn't do your homework.

The reality is that you will need at least a certain amount of cash to start your business. You might already have it in your bank; in that case, well done! But you might need to search for funding. That is why you need to know how much and by when.

***

A Word About VAT

There is one particular term you'll hear a lot, so it's essential you at least have a general grasp of what it means. VAT stands for 'valued added tax.' This tax is charged at a flat rate on a product or service you sell.

How you pay your VAT to the tax people depends on where you are in the world. This varies hugely, and you should probably consider getting some advice from an accountant. For example, you might pay your VAT returns every quarter or every month - it varies.

VAT is included in the price when you buy something, but as a business owner, when calculating your finances, including your 5-year projection and break-even point, these should all be done excluding VAT.

As a business owner, you will need to pay Value Added Tax (VAT) for the services/goods you purchased and collect VAT for the services/goods you sold. All of this must be reported to the government, what you paid and collected. The government will then let you know if you owe them money or if they owe you (that does happen, the government giving you money).

Most countries also have a VAT threshold; for instance, if you earn under a certain amount, you won't need to pay VAT, but the moment you go over that, you'll need to register and pay legally.

Again, if this is all super-confusing, have chocolate; it will lift your mood. And get your accountant involved. My goal here is that you are aware of VAT, and that is a good starting point.

***

Why You Need a Break-Even Calculator

Before you even dream of launching your business, you must know your break-even point. You will cover all your costs at this point, but of course, you won't make any money. Anything you sell beyond your break-even point is profit.

You can use a break-even calculator to make your life much easier, which is especially important when you're planning to sell physical products. These will incur a cost before you even sell them, and you'll need to know how much you need to shift before the money starts rolling into your bank account.

Of course, you can clear your budding headache easily by outsourcing this part; if you know someone who's pretty good with numbers, just ask them to help you. You might also be tempted to skip it, and if you want to, well, who am I to stop you? But it's good information to have, and it'll help you understand the sales you'll need to reach if you want to cover everything without losing money right off the bat.

So, while numbers could be a pain in the neck, just spend time on them, and your life will be easier. You have my permission to reward yourself with a glass of wine afterward!

When you break even, the total amount of your costs and your revenue are at an equal point. You're not gaining anything, but you're not losing anything, either. This is your baseline aim. Of course, you want to go beyond this point to start making a profit, but that comes a little later.

To work out your break-even point, you need to know your costs. There are two types: fixed costs and variable costs. Fixed costs are always the same, so we're talking about things like renting a shop for example. As the name suggests, your variable costs can vary depending on usage. The materials you need to buy to make your products are one. The more you sell, the more you need to buy to make the product. That is a variable cost.

To work out the point where your sales cover all your expenses, both fixed and variable, you can use this equation. As far as math goes, it's a pretty easy one:

Fixed Costs ÷ (Selling Price Per Unit - Variable Costs Per Unit) = Break-even point

If you head online, you can find calculators that will work all of this out for you. But knowing the equation helps you work out what you need to do. To put it simply, you need to make sure that you're selling enough so that you don't have to pay for your expenses out of your own pocket.

Let's look at an example to clear the fog from your brain.

Let's say that a company is creating cell phone cases. Their fixed costs come to $50,000 per month, which includes rent, wages, accounting software, etc. Their variable costs associated with creating their cases are $0.80 per unit (per phone case), and they sell their phone cases at $2 each. Remember, these prices should exclude the VAT.

50,000 ÷ (2.00-0.80) = 41,666 units need to be sold to break even. No profit is made at this point.

Now, that's a wild example, but it gives you an idea of how this works. The next question is what happens if your sales vary. After all, the market can dip sometimes, and maybe you don't sell 50,000 units every month. In that case, you'll need to start looking to save costs or have a buffer to help you in those months when something drastic happens. You can also consider increasing the price you sell your product for, therefore putting the burden on the customer. It happens all the time, but be careful with this one because you might then be overpriced.

5-Year Projection Plan

I know what you're thinking: 'How am I supposed to see five years into the future.' Don't sweat it. This doesn't have to be super-accurate!

The idea of a 5-year projection plan is that you can see a realistic and educated idea of what your business will be able to achieve in its first five years. If you intend to become a millionaire after one year, putting your 5-year projection plan into action will probably bring you back down to earth with a bump.

This plan helps you understand at which point you can break even, when you can start making a profit and how much of a profit you can realistically make. But remember, no crystal ball here, so it's not a 'to the point' record. Honestly, it's simply an estimation and something you can work with to give you an idea of where to go.

A 5-year projection plan is presented in a balance sheet format, so if you know any accountants, now is the time to get friendly with them if this is not your game. But don't skip it; you'll only be searching around in the dark, which is never fun.

A plan such as this is pretty beneficial on many levels:

- It helps you make financial decisions that won't immediately send you into the red.
- It allows you to see issues before they turn into major headaches.
- It gives you something to work with when you're deciding whether to hire or not.
- It helps you keep an eye on any contracts you have with vendors and whether you're getting value for money or not.
- It helps you assign money to certain things to avoid falling short in another area.

Creating such a plan keeps your feet on the ground and your head out of the clouds. Your market research will help you estimate how many units you expect to sell per month. From there, you can work out when you're likely to hit that golden break-even point. After that, you can work out a realistic time to start earning a profit.

Once your 5-year plan is sorted out, you'll know how much cash you'll need so you don't end up slipping and drowning in the red. That's never a good place to be. You'll also work out a suitable buffer for the months that are a bit slow. Remember, breaking even is your primary aim, anything less than that and your business will start costing you money rather than making it.

It's also important to know that you're not going to make a profit right off the bat. It will take a few months, maybe even years, depending on your business model, to break even, and then after that, you can start to work toward money in your bank account. Don't be discouraged if you're not making a profit after a few months. It is all part of the process.

What is the Gross Profit Margin Percentage?

You might have accidentally heard the term Profit Margin or GP% during dinner with friends or at the water cooler at work. It is used to calculate the profitability of your business or your products.

I hope your next question is. What does the math look like behind this magical number?

(Selling Price - Cost Price) ÷ Selling Price = Gross Profit % or GP%

This is also a relatively simple calculation, but it is always helpful to see it in action. So let's practice this.

I am going to use nice round numbers for this one. You have decided to sell your product at $10 (excluding the VAT), and buying or making it currently will cost you $5 (excluding the VAT).

Before we use the example above to calculate your GP%, we first have to go a little deeper into the cost price of your product.

Time to add up all the different parts of your product costs. The actual product price is only $2, but you have to ship it to your warehouse or physical store, which will cost you $2, plus you have to pay for packaging at $1. This is your nice round $5 cost price.

Finally, you are ready to do the math.

($10 - $5) ÷ $10 = 50%

It looks pretty simple, but you need to ensure you include all the different variables when calculating your Cost Price. Otherwise, you will undervalue the cost of your product and get a nasty surprise down the line.

Inventory Planning & Revenue

The first thing I want you to predict is how many monthly units you plan to sell. When you know that, you will learn how many you need on hand to have enough to sell.

The first month you need to buy stock, the chances of selling anything in the first month are relatively slim.

Suppose you plan to sell 1000 units in your first month of proper sales. You are thinking, great, I just need to buy 1000 units. But here is the kicker, you cannot just buy the 1000 units to cover your predicted sales. You will need some buffer because maybe everyone loves your product so much that you need a little more, and you don't want to run out of stock before you even start.

Instead, you need to buy 1500 units.

As your business grows and the months keep ticking, the units you plan to sell will increase! This is great! Exactly what you want. You also need to increase the amount of stock you purchase and make sure there is always a BUFFER.

Time to convert these into values and look at an example:

Units & Gross Profit	Months				
	1	2	3	4	5
Units Sold		1000	1000	1500	1500
Units Bought	1500	1000	1000	2000	2500
Sales/Revenue	$ -	$10 000	$10 000	$15 000	$15 000
Cost	$ 7 500	$ 5 000	$ 5 000	$10 000	$12 500
Gross Profit	$ -7 500	$ 5 000	$ 5 000	$ 5 000	$ 2 500

I hope you picked up what I did there. In months 4 and 5, we started to predict selling more, but at the same time, we increased the amount we bought.

The BIG Net Profit or Loss

The loss part does not sound great, but when you start out, this is very normal to see some months going in the red. When you start to break even and go beyond your break-even point regularly, this red number will be a beautiful green number.

You have your Gross Income. Well done! Now you have to deduct even more cost from that. Ugg!

These are the fixed costs we have mentioned in your break-even section. You must add all those random deductions, rent, phone bills, permanent wages, freelancers, accounting software, advertising, training cost, etc.

Now take your Gross Income and deduct the TOTAL of these expenses. This will give you your Net Income.

Let's have a look-see how this will look in your 5-year projection.

Net Profit/Income	Months				
	1	2	3	4	5
Sales/Revenue	$ -	$ 10 000	$ 10 000	$ 15 000	$ 15 000
Cost	$ 7 500	$ 5 000	$ 5 000	$ 10 000	$ 12 500
Gross Profit	$ -7 500	$ 5 000	$ 5 000	$ 5 000	$ 2 500
Marketing & Advertising	$ 100	$ 100	$ 100	$ 100	$ 100
Legal and professional fees	$ 100	$ 100	$ 100	$ 100	$ 100
Rent	$ 1 000	$ 1 000	$ 1 000	$ 1 000	$ 1 000
Wages	$ 1 000	$ 1 000	$ 1 000	$ 1 000	$ 1 000
Total Operating Cash Out	$ 2 200	$ 2 200	$ 2 200	$ 2 200	$ 2 200
Net Income/Profit	$ -9 700	$ 2 800	$ 2 800	$ 2 800	$ 300

Importance of a Cash Flow Statement

You thought you were done, right? You now need to add all your work together.

A cash flow statement summarizes the money coming in and going out of your business. Not just your sales and expenses but also things like investments, dividends, or loan repayments.

It's like a personal bank account but for a business. So, you just open a bank account. Currently, there is a big fat zero on your statement. It is payday, and you got your first money coming in. It looks beautiful and shiny. Time to celebrate! You go out with friends or family for a tasty dinner and splurge on some nice wine.

The next day everything still looked very positive. It is the first day of the month, and everyone wants your money, debit orders, loan repayments, rent, etc. Your phone doesn't stop pinning off those deductions coming from your account. Things are looking a bit gloomier by now. But you still have to eat for the rest of the month.

Suddenly halfway through the month, your car breaks, and you have no choice but to pay that bill. Without being prepared, your balance goes into overdraft just 2 days before your next payday. You are now a proper adult. Your opening bank account balance is negative.

Or maybe you have been taught well. You budget every month. Put savings away for those unforeseen expenses. And you don't buy everything you see. Good on you! You have a positive balance at the end of the month.

You need to do the exact same thing for your business, keep an eye on these opening and ending balances.

First, let us examine the fancy business terms and structure of this type of statement.

All things explained	Cash Flow Statement
Cash is like your bank account after a long weekend – it's a little bit lower than when you started! **opening cash Year 2 = ending cash of Year 1**	**Opening Cash**
You sold your Products!	Sales
There will always be customers that want their money back	Refunds
Discounts & Promotion will be part of your strategy	Discounts
This is turnover = sales - refunds - discounts	*Total Operating Cash in*
Your own money invested BUT keep some so you can eat while your business grows	Capital
The people who believed in your business, and those funds!	Financing
	Total Non-Operating Cash In
Sales + Funding	**Total Cash In**
You bought product, it will cost money	Cost of Goods Sold Excl VAT
All your stuff that you spend your money on	Marketing & Advertising
	Legal and professional fees
	Rent
	Wages
Add all your costs together	*Total Operating Cash Out*
No Loan is for Free	Loan Repayment + Interest
Depended on Country BUT only payable if your turnover hits a certain amount	Corporate Tax
	Total Non-Operating Cash Out
All cost + Loan repayment	**Total Cash Out**
Opening Balance + Total Cash In - Total Cash Out = Red or Green Bank Balance	**Ending Cash**

Next up practice time!

Cash Flow Statement	Months				
	1	2	3	4	5
Opening Cash	**$ -**	**$ 653**	**$ 1 806**	**$ 2 959**	**$ 4 012**
Sales		$ 10 000	$ 10 000	$ 15 000	$ 15 000
Refunds				$ -100	$ -100
Discounts		$ -1 000	$ -1 000	$ -1 000	$ -1 000
Total Operating Cash in	$ -	$ 9 000	$ 9 000	$ 13 900	$ 13 900
Capital	$ 1 000				
Financing	$ 10 000	$ -	$ -	$ -	$ -
Total Non-Operating Cash In	$ 11 000	$ -	$ -	$ -	$ -
Total Cash In	**$ 11 000**	**$ 9 000**	**$ 9 000**	**$ 13 900**	**$ 13 900**
Cost of Goods Sold Excl VAT	$ 7 500	$ 5 000	$ 5 000	$ 10 000	$ 12 500
Marketing & Advertising	$ 100	$ 100	$ 100	$ 100	$ 100
Legal and professional fees	$ 100	$ 100	$ 100	$ 100	$ 100
Rent	$ 1 000	$ 1 000	$ 1 000	$ 1 000	$ 1 000
Wages	$ 1 000	$ 1 000	$ 1 000	$ 1 000	$ 1 000
Total Operating Cash Out	$ 9 700	$ 7 200	$ 7 200	$ 12 200	$ 14 700
Loan Repayment + Interest	$ 647	$ 647	$ 647	$ 647	$ 647
Corporate Tax					
Total Non-Operating Cash Out	$ 647	$ 647	$ 647	$ 647	$ 647
Total Cash Out	$ 10 347	$ 7 847	$ 7 847	$ 12 847	$ 15 347
Ending Cash	**$ 653**	**$ 1 806**	**$ 2 959**	**$ 4 012**	**$ 2 565**

Tracking Your Plan

It's a good idea to have a monthly check-in with your projection plan to work out whether you're on track or if something needs to be tweaked. As you start making sales, you might notice that you have an expense you never planned for; in that case, you'll need to update your projection plan to cover that expense.

After a few months, you can then look to do a reforecast. Maybe your plan is on track, and you don't need to do anything. If that's the case, well done you. You're a rare case! It's far more likely that you'll need to tweak a few things, and that's okay. It's better to see it now and make an action plan than to discover it further down the line and wonder where you will magically find the extra money.

The longer you run your business, the more you'll become familiar with the reality of it. It's easy to plan when you're starting out, but your experience is limited. Once you've got real-life experience, you'll understand more about what you need.

***

Adapt, Adapt, And Adapt Some More

Throughout the whole thing, there's one thing you need to be: adaptable.

By being adaptable. It gives you the upper hand to change course according to situations as they arise, making you more likely to find innovative solutions to problems. And trust me, problems will crop up. They always do. It's like the business world loves to test your mettle for the sake of it.

Having a mindset of adaptability also means that you keep that slight emotional detachment that stops you from being too rigid. You might need to make a new plan after a few months because you realize the first one came from la-la land. If you're too rigid, you'll force it to work. And we all know that forcing something is never the right route.

Homework Time

If you're not a math fan, you've probably found this chapter difficult. It might even have made you second guess whether you want to start a business. Wait up! Numbers are an integral part of running a business. At the start, you'll need to deal with a lot of this on your own, but remember that those numbers won't be complicated forever, especially when you start making a profit.

It's more challenging initially because there is nothing to compare it to and then be able to make informed decisions. But after a few months, you will have, and that's when you can sit down and re-look at your plans. You can then make changes, try a new approach, or realize that you might be psychic after all.

So, what is your homework for this chapter?

- Do plenty of market research and determine how much you will charge for your product. Remember, don't undercharge, and don't overcharge. Look at what your competitors are charging and develop something that makes you competitive without losing out.

- Work out your break-even point. It's the most basic calculation you need for your business; you'll be lost without it. Take your time and test it a few times to ensure the figure you arrive at is the right one.
- Brainstorm some ideas on where you assume your business will be within five years, in line with the growth of other similar businesses. You can always look at the rise of your competitors and see how long it took them to start breaking even and making a profit. From there, you can create your 5-year projection plan.

Chapter Six

The Big Business Plan

There's a lot of planning going on right now, isn't there?

You might be getting impatient and wondering when the planning can stop, and the doing can start. Well, soon soon, but not quite yet.

To start a business properly and have even a tiny chance of getting any funding from a bank or investor, you need a business plan.

You can put it together yourself if you want to, and it's a good idea to try and do that and then look for help afterward if you feel it is needed. That way, the expert can tweak what you've written, and they'll have the information they need to deal with.

But we're getting ahead of ourselves.

First things first, let's talk about what a business plan is, what it includes, and why you need it.

***

Wait Up, What is a Business Plan?

We know that a 5-year projection plan is about the money side of things, but a business plan goes further. This is a formal document that outlines everything about the business. It includes what the business does, what it provides, what it's about, its values, how many people work there, how many people will work there in the future, a little about you as the owner, and what you plan to do as time goes on.

The aim here is that if you need to look for investors or go to the bank and ask for a business loan, they have an idea of what they're giving you money for. You need the documentation to back your plan up.

Every business needs a business plan, so don't even think about skipping this step. While it might sound time-consuming, it will give you some clarity about where you're going.

What should be in your business plan?

- Executive summary
- Company description
- Market analysis
- Organizational structure
- Funding request

- Financial plan
- Operating plan
- Risk management plan
- Appendix

Don't panic. I will talk about each one in turn in the coming sections.

First, you need a 'why.'

Why do you need a business plan exactly? Why do you need to sit down and plan your business like a psychic peering into the fog of a crystal ball? Well, there are a few good reasons.

- **Your business plan is like a GPS** - Consider your business plan as your sat-nav, only without the annoying voice. As you start to launch your business, you'll have so much going on, a million and one emotions, and you might find it easy to lose sight of what's going on. Your business plan will pull you back to the here and now and keep you on track.

- **You'll find it easier to reach your goals** - Making sound business decisions is easier if you know what you want to achieve and have already thought about how you will do it. Now, your plan isn't going to answer every single question you're ever going to have, but it will keep you true to your original aims and values. That can mean a lot when strong and perhaps controversial business decisions must be made.

- **The funding question** - One of the most significant aims of a business plan is to help you get funding when needed. You won't get a business loan from a bank if you just rock up and give them a story about what you want to achieve. They won't just take your word for it; they'll need to see plans on paper. Banks are annoying like that. The same goes for investors; would you give your money to someone who says they will make you rich and doesn't back it up? Probably not.

***

What Should Your Business Plan Look Like?

Typically, a business plan for a small business is about 15-20 pages long.

You're panicking, aren't you? Don't panic. You can put one section on each page, and trust me, that will pad it out quickly enough!

Your business plan is a key part of your business, so make sure it's easy to read and well laid out. If you need to present this to request funding from someone, they'll get bored if it's too long and technical and totally put off if it's too short and looks like a preschooler wrote it.

You need to sound like you know exactly what you're talking about, and you should add appendices at the end to include additional documents that give more kudos to your business idea and its chances of success.

However, home-based or Internet-based businesses probably won't have a business plan that runs to these many pages. It's more important to ensure you get all the information down than to become obsessed with page numbers.

Make sure the font is professional, there are no mistakes, such as dodgy typos, and it looks attractive without being 'pretty.' Remember, you're aiming for professional, not cute.

Then, your plan should be stored in a folder and collated in section order. Don't just have a random handful of a few pages and expect it to look like a professional business plan; instead, think of a professional report in a binder, and you're good to go.

Let's Get Rid of the Confusion: The Important Parts of a Business Plan

Each section of a business plan is important in its own right, so it's not a good idea to leave any of them out. Some sections might not be as important to your business as others, but there will still be key information you need to include. Covering everything shows potential investors that you're serious and covered all bases.

Let's look at each section in detail to reduce stress.

Executive Summary

This is perhaps the easiest part of your business plan. Basically, this is a summary of your business and what is included in your plan. It describes your business, its reason for existence, who you're targeting, and key financial points.

Every executive summary of a business plan is unique because every business is equally unique. But, to give you an idea of how an executive summary looks, let's check out a quick example.

"Super phones are an online cell phone accessories provider, offering bespoke cell phone cases for customers who send photographs of what they want to see included on their case. Customers want to feel like their phone is different from everyone else's, and bespoke cases fulfill that desire.

Super Phones' target customers enjoy spending time on their phones but like to accessorize and feel like they have something 'new'. Of course, buying a new cell phone is expensive, but a new case can make your phone feel brand new from the get-go. The cell phone accessories market was worth $250 billion in 2021, giving kudos to just how in demand these products are.

In the first three months after launch, Super Phones aims to earn in excess of $2000 in profits per month. The business is founded and run by Sylvia Smith, a professional graphic designer with eight years of experience."

Now, that's just a quickly pulled-together example, but it shows you the main points you need to put into your executive summary. Keep it simple; your business plan is a roadmap for both you and your investors. It's a reminder of why you started your business.

For all of those reasons, don't blind people (or yourself) with science and big words. Keep it simple and engaging. Think of it as the introduction to a book you want people to read.

Company Description

This one is pretty simple to understand. The company description is a description of the business, what it provides, its target customers, and its advantages over its competitors. You'll already have all of this information from your market research, so it's just a case of putting it into an engaging format.

"The idea for ClearSkin appeared from personal experience. Having searched for a completely natural moisturizing product for many years, I found nothing to suit my combination skin. I realized that if I wanted my ideal product, I would need to make it myself. Many existing products are drying, harsh on sensitive skin, and contain irritants that are unacceptable for many people with skin problems.

ClearSkin has created a 100% organic moisturizer with both cooling and soothing properties. The product promotes anti-aging while being suitable for people with specific skin issues, such as acne or eczema. All ingredients are free of added extras, such as parabens and sulfates. Products are cruelty-free and dermatologically tested.

ClearSkin's target audience is all age groups and those tired of not knowing what is included in their skincare products. By offering a completely natural option, customers can be assured that they're not worsening existing skin issues, including acne, eczema, sensitive skin, rosacea, and dry skin."

Again, that's a random example, but you can see that your company description is a little bit of a sales pitch. It's important not to make it sound too salesy; however, simply state the reasons why you chose to set up this business and the products/services you offer. Don't be afraid to outline personal experiences if they add extra kudos; it shows that you've done research both from your point of view and from the perspectives of others.

Market Analysis

Your market analysis summarizes your target market, any industry trends pertinent to your product/service range, and information about your competitors. Again, you already have this information, and this section is the opportunity for you to show that there is demand for your idea.

An excellent way to showcase your market analysis is via a SWOT analysis. That stands for strengths, weaknesses, opportunities, and threats. You can present this in a table format and even in bullet points to make it easier to read.

For example

Strengths:

- *Local demand for the product is high*
- *Many opportunities to expand the business via social media*
- *Low-cost materials available to keep overheads low*
- *Business can be run entirely online*

Weaknesses:

- *Pricing for materials is not competitive*
- *High competition in certain areas*
- *Postage costs*

Opportunities:

- *Social media marketing is a way to reach more people*
- *Branching out into bespoke printing from client photographs*
- *Custom items are currently in demand*

Threats:

- *Many competitors are using cheaper materials to undercut prices*
- *Increased postage costs could affect profits*

The SWOT analysis covers a lot of this section's needs and does so in an easy-to-read way. It also helps to add some information about your main competitors. That doesn't mean going into a full essay about their origins and what they do but naming them and giving a quick paragraph about what they offer and how you're different is enough.

Organization Structure

This section talks about who works for your business and their role. If you've not recruited yet, you can simply draw an organizational chart showing job roles and how they connect to one another.

It's important to carefully think about this before putting pen to paper. It's easy to assume you can do everything yourself, but can you really? You might save some cash, but you'll be so stressed out you won't have time for anything else - remember home and work-life balance!

It's much better to delegate some tasks to a junior staff member and pay them accordingly than to run yourself into the ground and perhaps the business itself. Plus, there are likely to be some tasks that you don't have a lot of knowledge in, but someone else is a super-expert that can help you and take the job off your hands.

Remember, pride comes before a fall.

So, what does your organizational structure need to look like on paper? An organizational chart is an easy way to show the structure of your business.

For example:

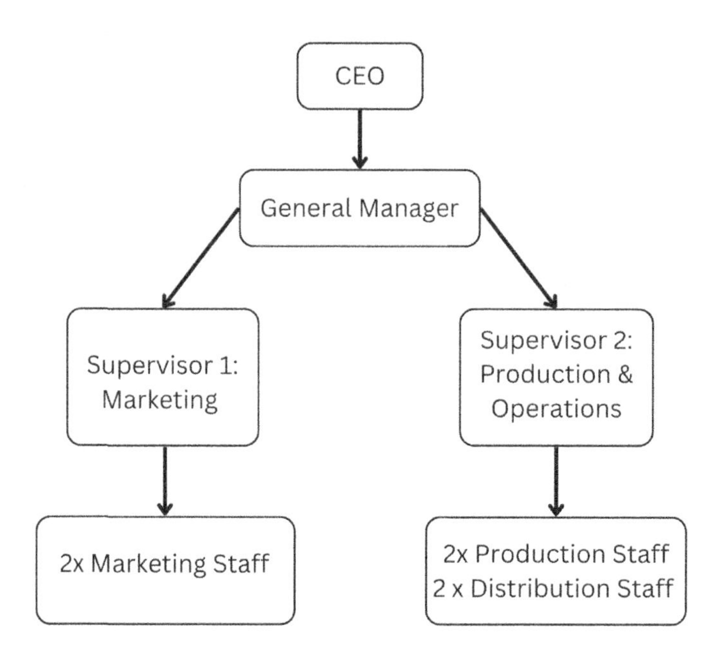

That may be wildly unrealistic, but a chart such as this shows who you need to work for you and their position in the organization. You can also add essential duties within the chart or list them below in bullet point format. However, don't go into too much detail; the reader doesn't need to know that your general manager will open the mail every day or that your marketing staff will dust their desks daily. Stick to the relevant stuff, and don't bore people!

In this section, you don't need to list everyone you ever envisage working for you because no crystal ball in the world will give you that information. You need to outline the critical personnel you need right now, over the coming months, and in the first couple of years. If you expand from there, great; you can create a new organizational chart then. For now, keep it simple.

Of course, it might be that there won't be other staff and it will just be you. In that case, you don't need to go all fancy and draw a chart, you can just list your responsibilities, and if you do hire at a later date, you can update this section accordingly.

Funding Request

As part of your financial planning in the last chapter, you'll know if you need extra funding or not. The chances are that you will, and, in that case, you can add a funding request to your business plan.

As the name suggests, this is a written request for future funding, usually covering the first five years of your business.

Now, this is where it gets tricky.

The first five years of a new business are pretty rocky, and it's likely that your launch will go through different stages. You might not need funding to get your business started, but you may need funding to move to the next stage of your plan. In that case, you'll need to outline when you expect that to be, what you will need, why, and how you plan to cover costs.

Of course, you might need funding even to start the business, i.e., now. In that case, you need to put more emphasis on the launch and how you can create a competitive edge from the get-go. Investors prefer to put money into a business that has had some success; it lessens the risk and gives them a better night's sleep, but that doesn't mean they're not keen to be a part of something new either. All you need to do is be as persuasive as possible without telling white lies.

Your funding request should include:

- How much funding you'll need, i.e., a ballpark figure.
- What type of funding do you need, e.g., short-term loan, long-term, etc.?
- What you're offering in return, e.g., part-ownership of the business, schedule of repayments, etc.
- Future plans. This is about what you will do with the money and how it will benefit the person lending you the cash. Be persuasive!

What if you don't need any funding at all? Well, you can thank your lucky stars and miss this section out completely!

Not everyone will need funding; if you're starting a dropshipping business or thinking of becoming a freelance writer, you might find that you don't need anything to get started, just a plan to do it. In that case, don't push funding options out of your mind completely. Maybe at some point in the future, you will need to think about it if your business grows sufficiently. However, depending on how well things are going, you might be able to cover those costs from your income.

Funding requests are often necessary when setting up a larger-scale business, such as a brick-and-mortar shop. Business plans aren't designed to be 'one size fits all,' so if this section isn't pertinent to you, it's perfectly fine to miss it out for now and include it later on.

Financial Plan

This section of your business plan comes down to number crunching, but it's not as complicated as it seems. Thanks to your earlier calculations, you'll already have all of this information sorted out.

Your financial plan is just an overview of where you're currently at financially speaking and projections for the coming months and years. It's telling whoever reads your business plan about how you expect growth to go based on market research and your own (realistic) aspirations.

You can make this section as detailed as you want, but it's a good idea to put at least several sections in so that you can show any potential investors or the bank that you're serious about what you're doing and have everything planned out.

Your financial plan should include:

- Short-term perspectives and long-term prospects, i.e., what you expect to happen and how you expect growth to go
- The potential for profit over three months, six months, one year, and beyond
- Your current financial situation, e.g. if you have the capital or you're seeking it
- An outline of startup costs
- A projected balance sheet (you can get help with this from your accountant or a friend who's savvy with numbers)

- Your previous break-even analysis should go in this section too

Operating Plan

The operating plan is a detailed outline of how your business will go about it. You'll cover daily tasks that allow you to meet your customer's needs and how each person contributes toward the business objectives.

Obviously, this part of your plan is a lot easier if only you are working there, but if you have a few people, you'll need to explain their duties and how they all work together to reach the end goal - making the customer happy.

This part also needs to talk about marketing and how you'll get the word out to the masses about whatever you're offering. You can easily break this into subsections to make creating your operating plan easier.

You should cover:

- **Preparation** - How you'll prepare for your goods or services to be created, i.e., sourcing materials, putting them together, and purchasing what you need to offer a service.

- **A rundown of the work chain** - This section covers who is responsible for what. So, if it's just you, you'll run through the process of taking an order from a customer, creating the product/service, sending it out (if necessary), and how you'll receive payment.

- **Marketing** - How are you going to market your goods and services? Here you can talk about things like social media marketing, if you're going to use any printed advertisements, etc. What is your marketing plan, and who is responsible for it?

- **Logistics** - This section is about how you'll get your goods/services to the customer. If you're using a courier company, state who they are, the prices you'll have to pay, and how the customer will absorb those through your pricing strategy. If you're providing an actual service in a place, you'll explain where the service will be carried out, e.g., in your salon, etc.

- **Customer service** - Here, you can talk about what you'll do if a customer wants to return one of your goods. How will they do that? Who can they contact if they have any problems, and what is your complaints procedure? How many days will you give people to return goods for a full refund? What if they try to return them after that time?

The operating plan might sound obvious, but by being as detailed as you can be here, you're showing potential funding sources, how you've thought your entire strategy out, and you've covered all areas that need covering. Also, by doing this, you're almost thinking ahead of the game because you can think about any potential problems before they arise and how you'll overcome them.

Risk Management

No one expects you to see the future and identify every single risk or thing that might go wrong in your business, but you do need to think about the obvious things you'll need to plan for. Your risk management section could include a list of issues you've identified and how you will get around them.

Without being all doom and gloom, you need to sit down and brainstorm the possible risks that could affect your business. By that, I mean what might happen that causes you a problem?

I know, I know - anything could happen. But that's not what we're thinking about here; we're thinking of real risks that could affect how your business runs. So, don't allow your mind to start over-analyzing everything; just stick to the realistic issues that could cause your business to run less smoothly.

Once you've identified a risk, you need to run through the stages of risk management. They are:

- **Define the risk** - State the risk clearly and get it clear in your mind.
- **What is the risk** - What adverse effects will the risk cause?
- **Monitor the risk** - How can you keep an eye on it and stop it from snowballing?
- **Actions to manage the risk** - What actions can you take to fix the risk?
- **Monitor your actions** - How can you monitor your actions to ensure they're working?

- **Assess the risk again** - Now you've taken extra steps, are they enough, or do you need to do more?

Let's run through an example to see how this works.

Let's say you've identified a risk relating to postage/shipping. Obviously, long delays will annoy your customers and could lead them to do business elsewhere. That's a problem.

So, you've **defined the risk** by stating what it is and worked out **the effects it will have** on your company. That's the first two steps done.

You then decide that a delay is anything over five working days, and you can **monitor that risk** by checking tracking information with the delivery company. That's how you monitor the risk.

If you notice that a delivery is delayed, what **actions can you take** to manage the risk? You can chase up the delivery company and find out how long the shipment will take, obtaining a firm ETA. You can then call the customer and apologize profusely, giving them an ETA of when to expect their order, and you could provide them with a percentage off their next order as a sweetener.

Next, you need to **monitor your actions**. You can continue to track the shipment, keeping an eye on any further delays, and you can call the customer again to confirm delivery and, once again, apologize for the delay.

Once the issue has been resolved, you must continue assessing **the risk**. You can do that by keeping a log of how often shipments are delayed, and if you think it's becoming too much of a problem, you can look into alternative shipping companies with better reputations.

And that's it!

You'll need to repeat that process in your business plan for every realistic risk you identify, but don't go overboard; just stick to the most likely issues. You don't want to present a business plan with ten pages of potential problems to a potential investor. Yes, you've figured out how to fix them, but it's not the best first impression!

Appendix

Think of the appendix as a folder of documents that don't fit anywhere else but are still important enough to be mentioned. That's what this section is for. It's supporting documents and information that can help a person understand the business plan and your business in general.

I'm talking about things like graphs, tables, and charts that add extra information to anything you've already mentioned. In your business plan, you can leave a small note (just use a superscript with a number and add a note in the footer) telling the person to look in the appendix at documents x, y, or z.

You can also add here any existing contracts you have with clients or other vendors you'll use, any trademark documents or licenses you'll need, and visual illustrations of your products or samples of your packaging.

Anything you think will add value can be placed in this section.

***

Homework!

Writing a business plan is a pretty hefty task. I suggest breaking it up into bite-sized chunks and taking your time on each section.

Many people prefer to write their business plan themselves because they can put more of their heart and soul into it. They know the business better than anyone and want to explain it in as much detail as possible.

If that's how you feel about it, and it's probably a good thing if you do, then take your time creating your plan and reach out for advice when and if you need it.

So, what homework can you do to enhance your understanding of this rather bumper chapter?

- Take a look online at business plan templates and research how you would like to lay your plan out. When you have a template, you'll find it easier to fill in the gaps.
- Take several pieces of paper and write a separate business plan heading at the top of each; a page for organizational structure, a page for financial plan, etc. Then, brainstorm what you want to add to each section. Go back to this every few days for a week, and add whatever else comes to mind.
- Ask a business person you trust, a knowledgeable friend, or even a freelancer who understands business plans to review your draft plan before you finalize it.

Chapter Seven

Give Me Money, Money, Money!

Here is the truth, no matter how simple your business idea is, you'll probably need some cash at some point. How much depends heavily on your business model, what you want to do, and how you want to do it.

For example, you might want to start up a professional dog-walking service. It sounds like all you need is a decent fitness level, right? Well, you do need that, but you'll also need a little cash to market your services, even if it is just for business cards or flyers.

On the other hand, if your business model is quite large, such as opening a brick-and-mortar store or selling a physical product, you'll need a decent chunk of start-up cash. You need to buy the products you want to sell, pay rent/mortgage, market your goods, and this goes down to things like how you're going to package the goods, such as paper bags, etc.

The first step in deciding how much start-up cash you might need is writing down every single cost that you'll need to cover. That will give you a ballpark figure of what you need before you start making money. Of course, you have done all of this work in the break-even and 5-year projection section, so make sure you have that on hand.

You probably already have a good idea of what this business idea of yours is going to cost you, but it doesn't hurt to sit down and brainstorm everything so you're not missing something important. However small it seems, write it down.

***

Wait, Wait! What is Capital, Exactly?

Okay, let's double back for a second. You've probably heard the word 'capital,' and you're wondering why it equates to business. Yes, capital is about cities, but it can also be about money.

In this sense, capital is the money you need to start your business. However, as you establish your business, capital can also be other things you have, e.g., assets. A brick-and-mortar store you paid for is an asset, and therefore that's capital. In effect, it's money tied up in something else (property in this case) because you could sell it and get the cold, hard cash at some point if you wanted to.

There are many terms you'll hear thrown around related to all of this, such as capital assets, equity, blah, blah, blah, but seriously, don't overload yourself. You're not working on Wall Street, and you don't need to understand all of that right now. Let's hope you never have to!

***

Why You May Need Start-up Capital

Okay, so why might you need to find some startup capital to fund your new business idea?

Well, you may not have money in a savings account that you're free to do whatever with, and you need to find someone who will give you a helping hand. That can be either through an investor or via a loan from the bank. You might also decide to take on a business partner who can help fund your business idea.

However, know that when you seek financial help from an investor or a business partner, you'll need to give them something in return. Nothing in life is free, after all.

In this case, they'll own a share of the business. Investors don't generally have anything to do with the business's day-to-day running; they simply profit from what you're doing thanks to the money they gave you to get the whole thing off the ground at the start. However, business partners may want to get into the nitty-gritty of the operational side of your business. Not always, but sometimes.

If you don't want this, you can look for what is called a 'silent partner.' Here, a silent partner will be your partner in business, but they won't have anything to do with how the business is run or what you're planning to do, and they won't give their ideas about how you might like to improve something or change something up. Basically, they keep their mouths shut; hence they're silent.

Now, having a regular business partner could be a good thing if you're a little inexperienced and want someone on hand to give you advice. Having someone by your side with input may be useful to you, but it could be that they try to take over a little too much, and you're left with all the stuff you don't want to deal with.

It's something you'll need to think about very carefully before deciding. So, without further ado let's jump into the pros and cons of finding capital from different sources.

Startup Capital Options - Pros & Cons

There are different options you can look at when you're trying to find a way to fund your business. In this section, I'm going to talk about some of the most common options and give you the pros and cons of each. That way, you can find a suitable option that is best for you and your business model.

Remember, there is no right or wrong here; it's a totally personal choice.

Bootstrapping

Now, bootstrapping has nothing to do with actual boots. All this means is that you're funding your business startup yourself, be it through credit card usage or your savings. In essence, you're covering your costs out of your pocket to fund your business for the first few months until you start to see a profit.

Something to consider, are you okay with not having access to them for a while because you'll have invested them in your business? After all, it will probably be a while before you see money in your bank account; that means it will be a while before you can put your savings back.

Think about if it is more sensible to look for outside funding options and keep your savings as a buffer. You never know what might happen in the future, and that's generally what we have savings for in the first place.

So, what are the pros and cons?

Pros

- You don't owe money to anyone else from the get-go.
- You may start to see a profit sooner because you don't have to add in any payments to loans etc., from the start.
- You can access your funds quickly, and you don't have to spend time wooing investors or applying for loans, which can be time-consuming and stressful.

Cons

- Growth may be limited because your funding will have a limit, too, i.e., your personal wealth.
- You may become too emotionally attached to your business because you've funded it, therefore clouding your judgment when making decisions.
- You may lose everything. Sorry to say, but it's something to consider. Which is a pretty significant risk for most of us.

- Bootstrapping may not be an option for you from the start.

Borrowing From Friends or Family Members

Another viable option is to borrow money from close friends or family members and pay it back (if they want it back) over time. However, there is a risk here, too; what if you borrow money from a friend or family member, and the business goes under pretty quickly? Again, not being negative here, but it's something you have to think about. Will you be in a position to give them back their money at some stage?

Mixing business with pleasure is a risky thing. While some friends and family members may understand, others might not. Of course, you could give them part ownership in the business in exchange for their money, but perhaps that's not something you want to mix either.

Consider this one carefully, but there are upsides and downsides here too.

Pros

- If all goes well, someone you care about will benefit as well as you.
- You can access money quickly in this case.
- You could offer part ownership to friends and family members.
- Trust is already there, so you don't need to spend time building that up, as you would with a regular investor.

- A friend or family member may be more lenient with paying things back (but not always).

Cons

- If your business doesn't do as well as expected, you may feel guilty on a personal level.
- Capital may be limited, depending on how much funding you can find this way.
- Mixing business and pleasure can be tricky and may complicate things between you.
- You may need to involve a lawyer to keep things amiable, which may cloud judgment and make you feel awkward about your personal relationship.

Business Partner

Enlisting the help of a business partner, either silent or otherwise, is a popular way to raise capital and tap into another person's ideas. This can be incredibly useful for a first-time business owner, but of course, it also means that you have to give them a cut of the profits and perhaps even a say in how things are run.

Pros

- Easy access to capital to help get your business off the ground faster.
- Faster growth due to two heads being better than one.
- You can tap into the other person's experiences, helping

you to make better decisions via collaboration.

- If you opt for a silent partner, they won't have any say in the running of the business, but you still utilize their capital.
- You can use your business partner's networking connections; it's not what you know but who you know!

Cons

- If you are going to allow your business partner to have a say in the business, you need to ensure that you're on the same page as this person from the start. Otherwise, you're looking at issues further down the road.
- You will need to draw up a contract with lawyers to ensure everything is laid out in terms of what both partners can and cannot do and the cut of the profits they can take.
- A business partner may insist on a higher cut of the profits if they invest a large sum of money from the start.

Small Business Loan

A small business loan is probably one of the most used types of capital for a small start-up business, and providing your business plan is solid. You can demonstrate that you've done your homework. It's probably one of the easiest ways to fund your business.

However, rates vary, and it's important to shop around and find a deal that suits you. That will also depend upon what the bank is willing to lend you, according to your personal situation and any debt-related history that you have.

Pros

- You'll have access to the money you need quickly after approval.
- The bank you borrow from won't want to be involved in your business and how it's run; they just want you to pay the money back!
- Some loans may offer you very good rates, so it's worth shopping around.

Cons

- You will need to pay back the monthly installments on time and with interest regardless of whether you're making a profit or not.
- Applications for loans can often be lengthy and time-consuming.
- The rate you're offered might not be what you want.
- Your business plan must be solid to be offered a loan like this.

Angel Investors

Not actual angels, although if they agree, you might think they are! An angel investor is a wealthy person who basically invests for fun or as their full-time job. They like to get involved with startup businesses and watch for growth. What a job to have!

The good thing about angel investors is that for a small business, you could have enough start-up cash and not need any other investors. You can find angel investors online by checking websites that give listings of individuals. From there, you'll need to reach out with your business plan and set up a meeting to discuss everything in detail.

Pros

- Angel investors are often business owners themselves or retired, so they've got a lot of knowledge and experience you can use to help in running your own business and making strong decisions.
- Angel investors are seen as a less risky alternative to venture capital (more on that shortly) because they don't have to answer to anyone else.
- Access to funds immediately after the contract has been drawn up.

Cons

- This person knows about investments, so you'll have to know your stuff and impress them pretty well.
- Angel investors often want to have a say in the running of the business, but not always. Make sure you iron this out before anything is signed.
- You'll need the help of a lawyer to draw up an airtight agreement that covers everything.

Venture Capital Investors

This is where business speaks comes into it! Venture capital investors are firms that invest in startup businesses to help get them off the ground in exchange for equity, i.e., they own a share of your business in relation to how much they invested.

However, don't push aside this idea from that rather scary-sounding explanation! Venture capital investors can often invest large amounts, so you can get what you need to grow quickly.

However, venture capital firms have an agenda - they want to grow your business so that it's big enough to be bought out in the future, and they can get a big chunk of cash. So, that's something to bear in mind, especially if that's not the direction you want your business to go in.

Pros

- Access to large amounts of capital.
- Investors have done this many times before and have much experience. That means they can help you with decision-making and problem-solving.
- The investor is looking to grow your business and help you look for reinvestment in the future - this could be a pro or a con for you, however.

Cons

- Investors will have a say in the business; the more they invest, the more of a say they will have. That could mean difficulty in making decisions and you have to relinquish a decent amount of control.

- These types of investors are often looking for tech start-ups, which could be an issue for you.
- Many see venture capital investment as risky because of the control that needs to be given and the lack of total, or maybe even majority, control.

Crowdfunding

You've probably heard of crowdfunding before, and it's growing in popularity. However, to attract investors from all walks of life and all corners of the world, you need to sell your stuff, i.e., your business plan! People can quickly get excited about an idea, but they will need to know that you're worth investing in.

Basically, you'll sign up for a crowdfunding website and look for investment from individuals. You'll do this by selling your product or idea to them and discussing it from there. It's a good option because it allows you to find multiple investors and, therefore, larger amounts of cash, but it can get messy with so many people involved. When people donate cash to your business endeavor, you'll move toward your target amount set when you sign up. If you reach this aim, you will receive the funds. If you don't? No funds come your way.

Of course, that's a big waste of time, so crowdfunding is only a good option if you can sell your idea and get people interested.

Pros

- You can receive funds from multiple people, giving you

access to larger sums.

- Anyone can invest in your business, not only accredited investment companies or individuals.
- You can use crowdfunding to build interest in your product and attract customers at the same time as looking for financial backing.
- It's relatively easy to get started and can be done from the comfort of your home - no scary business meetings!

Cons

- If you don't reach your financial goal when signing up, you won't receive any money. Basically, your hard work will be for nothing.
- You may not benefit from expertise because anyone can invest; they don't need business experience.
- The fact that anyone can invest also means that you haven't had a chance to research them as individuals, which could cause problems further down the line.

All of these options are viable and useful. It depends on which one fits you the best. For instance, if you want to start the dog-walking business we discussed earlier, you're probably not going to look at venture capital investments or even angel investments! You'll look at bootstrapping, family or friend lending, or perhaps a small business loan.

However, suppose you're looking to open a brick-and-mortar store to offer online sales simultaneously. In that case, you might need larger amounts of capital, which means venture capital firms, loans, or angel investments could be a better choice.

Do your research and go with what feels right to you. If you don't want to borrow huge amounts of cash at this point, don't. But also, don't sell yourself short either.

And remember the ability to lend all hinges on your business plan. Make it as solid as possible, and you'll have fewer questions to answer and more kudos to barter with.

It can be daunting to start looking for capital for your business but see this as a positive step. You've now got a plan in place, and you're making headway into getting your business off the ground. You may not get a solid 'yes' from the first person you speak to about investing in your business if, indeed, you go down that route, but keep at it.

After all, if you don't ask, you don't get it!

***

Homework Time!

We've talked about the pros and cons of different funding options, but how do they stack up against your personal business plan? Your homework for this chapter is to take each funding option we've talked about in this last section and write your own pros and cons list based on your business.

Doing this will help you understand which option is the best one for you and which may limit you to a point you're not comfortable with.

What's right for one business will be totally wrong for another. That's why choosing a funding option is so important. Don't just go for the easiest one either; it's always worthwhile hedging your bets and thinking carefully before making a choice. The phrase 'too good to be true' is often real.

For that reason, spending some time weighing up the pros and cons is a worthwhile task.

Chapter Eight

All Things Accounting & Legal

Right, let's get into it.

There are the pretty, shiny parts of starting a business and the complicated, dull parts. Unfortunately, you can't have one part without the other, and in this chapter, we're going to talk about a part of starting a business that many people don't relish. However, if you don't pay enough attention, you will find yourself in extremely hot water. The worst-case scenario is that you won't have a business at all.

But, if you focus on the positives, you can run through this section and feel like you're making serious headway into getting your business off the ground. In fact, you'll finally feel like a fully-fledged business owner. Pat yourself on the back!

I am, of course, talking about all things legal and anything related to accounting.

The next phase of starting a business involves dealing with lots of paperwork and bureaucracy. This might be painful, but with patience and perseverance, you'll eventually be ready to move on to the more exciting aspects of your business.

In this chapter, I want to talk to you about the things you 100% need to cover before you move any further with setting up your business. You've done a lot so far but are not quite there yet. The Government and other related agencies need to know about what you're doing so they can take a cut of your cash; sad but true. And if you don't register with the people you need to register with, the consequences will be horrific.

But these processes have been made simpler over the last few years, and plenty of online resources can help you do what you need to do without having to stand in office queues and wish you were somewhere else entirely.

So, take a deep breath, make yourself comfortable, and let's get on with it.

Don't Let Feeling Overwhelmed Stop You Right Now!

It's common for people to get this far into starting a business, and once they look at the list of things they need to do to register their business and get started, they decide it's too much trouble.

Making sure that you cover all bases is hard work, and when you're unsure how to do something or who you need to contact to get a particular piece of paper, it can seem like a massive mountain to climb. But think about how far you've already come. Don't give up now!

This can be an overwhelming part of the whole business deal but remember your 'why' and your passion. That will be enough to push you through and figure it all out. And if it helps, break it down into small chunks and tick each one off your list before moving on to the next. That way, you won't get totally strung out by having to fix a million and one things at once.

Slow and steady wins the race here, and it's not a competition anyway. A million people have done this before you, so it's totally doable, no matter how much drama it seems right now. Plus, a little challenge every now and then makes life exciting, right?

Just don't think it will never work for you just because you're facing what is probably your first major challenge. This is just paperwork, and paperwork is famously annoying. It's the same for everyone.

A Word About Geography

Before we get into the specific pieces of paper and registrations you need to obtain, it's important to remember that every country will have specific rules, guidelines, and procedures. That means you need to research what you need in your particular country and not assume that it will be the same as anywhere else. Often, small nuances make all the difference, and you'll only waste your time by not doing your research at this point.

You can also outsource portions of the process. But be careful when doing this because you need to know in your mind that every box has been ticked. Keep a close eye on your progress, and don't let some things fall through the cracks. If one thing is missed here, it could be a major issue further down the line, and that's a headache nobody needs.

Also, remember to shop around regarding certain things, such as insurance. You can get good deals that way; don't always take the first thing you're offered without knowing there's nothing better out there.

Finally, the Internet is full of many amazing things, but some are less than reliable at best, and highly questionable at worst. For that reason, only use popular and reputable websites, such as Government sites and things like Forbes. That is where you'll find the best information and again, make sure it's country-specific and not outdated.

To entirely cut out any doubt, there will always be a helpline number you can call and speak to someone directly. That way, you can ask any questions you need answers to and quickly move on from there.

***

Accounting - DIY or Let Someone Else Handle It?

Okay, let's cover one last question. Should you do your accounting yourself, or should you ask someone to do it for you? It's something most business owners question before they start and try to weigh up the pros and cons.

In all honesty, it's a personal choice. If you feel you can do it yourself and want to save money on paying someone, you can purchase the right software and do it on your computer. The best accounting software will do all the calculations for you and will keep the record you need to keep. It's a case of learning how to use the software package and nothing more. Even professional accountants use these software packages.

But, if you're not that computer savvy or you don't have the time, it's totally fine to outsource this to a freelance accountant. There is a lot you need to remember when it comes to accounting, even for a small business of just one or two people, and lots of records you'll need to keep in case of tax audits in the future. If you prefer to free up your mind to focus on other aspects of getting your business off the ground, then rather get a professional.

Of course, if you're already pretty savvy with accounting, you already know the answer to this question anyway!

I will also talk about accounting software a little more in the coming sections, so stay tuned for more on that.

Business Names

This might seem out of place, but before you can cover red tape and register where you need to register, you will need to give your business a name.

First things first, you need to brainstorm a few ideas. Maybe you already know, and in that case, you can skip this step. Remember that you'll be stuck with this name for a long time to come, so make sure it resonates with you. It needs to be easy to spell and pronounce and not something that is too closely related to anything icky-sounding. People notice.

And go for something unique, but don't make it weird. It's got to be memorable, but not for all the wrong reasons. Having said that, being too boring isn't a good idea either.

Who said naming your business was easy?!

It's vital that you don't choose a name that sounds anything like one of your competitors. There are rules against this, which doesn't help with your marketing strategy either. But aside from that, you need to check that your chosen name isn't already in use. You can do that by heading online and searching for registered business names in your area, state, or even wider area. If the name is free, you can use it. If not, you'll have to think again.

Then, you need to register it so that nobody else steals it from you. How to do that varies from state to state and country to country, so make sure you find the information you need and follow all the steps to the letter.

***

The Red Tape You Need to Cover

So, let's go through each piece of red tape you need to cut as you move closer to getting your business off the ground. It might be useful for you to write each of these down and tick them off as you go along so you know you've not missed anything, or just print this page out and keep it handy in your bag.

But again, remember to check what you need for your country. This is a very general list, and you may need extras depending on where you are in the world. It might also be that some of the terms used here aren't what these documents are called in your country, but you can research that and find the correct name, helping you on your way.

Business License

You may or may not need a business license, but it's vital that you check. It depends on the type of business you're running and where you're located as to whether you'll need one or not, but don't just assume. Most businesses need at least something, while larger businesses will need more.

Put simply, a business license is a type of approval or permit that the Government issues you with and allows your business to run within its limitations, i.e., a jurisdiction. Anything beyond that isn't allowed, so be sure to double-check before you expand your company!

Not having a license when you need one or going over the limitations of your license can result in harsh penalties and serious hot water in terms of your business operations.

Of course, it may be that you don't need a license, or you only need a specific type, and the best way to find out is to check ahead of time. This varies from country to country, but if you're in the US, you can check with the Secretary of State office for your particular state or a Department of Revenue. The US Small Business Administration also has a handy online tool that gives you the necessary information.

But again, this is only for the US. You need to find out your particular rules and ensure the information is correct. I can't stress this enough!

It's always better to make the call and get the information you need rather than just listening to someone who knows someone, who knows a person who ... you get the picture.

Tax ID Number

Everyone has to pay taxes, so this is one piece of red tape you will certainly need. In your country, it may not be called a tax ID number, it might be a company unique taxpayer reference (UTR), EIN, or something else entirely, but it's usually straightforward to find out via a quick online check.

Once you work out what the number is actually called, you'll simply need to apply to your local tax department, either in person or online, depending on the regulations where you are. You'll then be issued with the number you need to pay tax (boo) and complete other financial transactions as required throughout the life of your business. This will also be something you need for your accounting processes too.

It goes without saying that you will need to keep this documentation safe because it's super-important for the running of your business.

***

Accounting Software

If you're going to do your accounting yourself, you'll need to find the right software package to allow you to calculate everything you need and store records digitally. This is a major plus point because it means you don't have endless paper copies of everything lying around. Nobody has that much space, after all.

Then, when you need to pull off your year-end figures for tax purposes, you can just run the report you need, and you'll have those magic numbers right there. You can also pull up all sorts of other useful reports whenever you need them.

Trust me; accounting software has become a lifesaver for so many business owners and even for accountants themselves. Everything is stored digitally, and you no longer need endless box files with alphabetized records. It makes life ten times easier and gives you so many options for finding the data you need. Technology truly is a wonderful thing!

But of course, you'll need to shop around and find a package that suits your budget but also one that you click with. Perhaps download some free trials and have a play before deciding which package to go for. It's just like with Microsoft Word; not everyone likes it, and some people find they prefer Google Docs or vice versa. It comes down to what you prefer to use and how you get along with it.

However, there are a few well-known packages you can look into first, including QuickBooks, Sage Business Cloud, Xero, GnuCash, and Odoo. This isn't an exhaustive list, but these are some of the most popular.

The best accounting software packages don't only run reports when you need them, but they allow you to make sure that your books are all in order and that you can keep track of your sales, expenditure, and other important figures. That is information you can use in the first precious few months and years of your business as you look to reach break-even and then grow past that point.

You'll also need a good Internet connection as all your financial information is stored in the 'cloud.' It's all super-secure; nobody else can access it without the password and lots of other security information to input.

But, if you're not thinking of doing your own accounting, this is the point where you need to start looking for a company or freelancer to do it for you. Again, shop around, and don't just opt for the first person who holds up their hand and says, "Me! I'll do it!"

Remember, this is an integral part of your business, and you need to trust the person who runs your accounting for you. Look at their experience and qualifications, check reviews, and see how many other people they're working for: do they have time for another client? Don't be afraid to ask questions; the best accountants will expect it and have all the answers ready.

***

Business Bank Account

This is a piece of advice I cannot stress enough. Never be tempted to keep your business running through your personal bank account. Not only does it complicate matters, but in many ways, you need a business account to take advantage of business-related perks.

When looking for potential investors at the start or in the future, you'll need to show bank statements to prove your income from your business. If it's all mixed up with your personal bank account, the potential investor isn't going to want to see your shopping bill from Walmart that week or the receipt from the meal you had two weeks earlier.

Not only does it look unprofessional, but it will be impossible to keep track of everything, and you'll end up spending money from 'pots' you want to keep separate. By opening a business bank account, you can separate your personal spending and business operations.

This is another case of shopping around. There are countless banks no matter where you are in the world, and they all offer business accounts. Some have better perks than others, reasonable rates, extra services, etc. By doing some homework beforehand and knowing what you want, you can go and make an appointment with the bank and get the account you want. In some cases, you can even do it all online.

Remember that your bank account should make life easier so choosing the added extras to do that for you is something worth taking a little time over. Even something as simple as a small overdraft could be the buffer you need in the first few months of getting your business started.

Legal Advice

Look, Google can only get you so far in life. It's unfortunate, but it's true. And when it comes to anything legal, you shouldn't rely on something you read online alone.

As a business owner, you have certain obligations to meet, and there are also lines that you cannot cross from a legal point of view. The only way to get the correct information, according to where you are in the world and the type of goods and services you want to provide, is to talk to a lawyer. That way, you'll understand not only your obligations but the point where you cannot go any further.

If you don't have this information, it's easy to make a mistake. The only problem is, in the eyes of the law, mistakes aren't an excuse for anything. If you didn't know you were doing something wrong, it wouldn't matter; it isn't any type of defense legally. If anything, it shows you in a poor light because you didn't do your homework and find these things out beforehand.

It won't be a huge deal; simply shop around to find a lawyer who specializes in your particular area and one that fits your budget. Then, make an appointment and go and talk through everything. It's a good idea to write a list of any questions you have before you go, so you can make sure you cover everything you need to. That way, you won't kick yourself afterward and wish you'd asked something. Another appointment will only cost you more!

During your time with your lawyer, it's a good idea to talk about contracts and get the advice you need in that regard. Again, this all depends on your business idea; maybe you won't need contracts, and in that case, you have one less thing on your to-do list. But if you do, legal advice will help you avoid costly mistakes in the future.

A few possible contracts you might need to discuss include:

- **Operating Agreement** - This document outlines the ownership structure of the business and the management structure too. It's an excellent document to have because it outlines who is responsible for what, even going down to each role and its key responsibilities. This document also outlines voting rights and how decisions are made within the business. Suppose you have several people within your business, especially shareholders and business partners. In that case, this document can help to keep everything running smoothly and avoids conflicts over who is responsible for what. There are no shirking responsibilities when it's down in black and white!
- **Employment Agreement** - If you have employees, you'll

need a contract for each. This document outlines the employee's salary, work hours, duties, and any benefits they will receive. It also covers what happens in the event of termination of employment.

- **Non-disclosure Agreement** - This is a good option if you outsource anything, especially if you use freelancers. This agreement states confidentiality agreements cannot be shared or disclosed outside the working arrangement. For instance, if you hire a freelance writer to create some promotional material for you and give them access to your business information to help them in their role, they're not allowed to share that with anyone else. After all, you don't want important information getting into the hands of your competitors, do you?

- **Partnership Agreement** - If you have any partnerships within your business, e.g., a business partnership, you will need this document to protect both parties. This contract outlines what the partnership actually is, covering the structure of the business and how the partnership fits in, who owns the business and to what degree, the management structure, and what happens with profits.

- **Lease Agreement** - If you rent property from an owner, i.e., opening a brick-and-mortar shop, you'll need a lease agreement. This is a contract between the landlord and tenant that details the terms of rental, covering rent price, situations when the contract can be terminated, amount of notice required, etc. If at some point in the future you rent any property out to someone as your business grows, then you will need to provide your new tenant with this agreement.

- **Licensing Agreement** - If you're going to share anything in your business with someone else, e.g., a vendor, then you can issue them with a licensing agreement that basically grants them the rights to use your information or property in exchange for a fee/other types of compensation. An example could be an advertisement or a piece of writing you create; in that case, the other person would need to compensate you if they use it.

- **Vendor Agreement** - You may or may not use outside vendors; if you do, you'll need this agreement too. This contract outlines what the vendor will provide you with, the limitations of that provision, how much you will pay, and deadlines.

- **Business loan agreement** - If you take out a business loan, getting your lawyer to look over it before you sign on the dotted line is a good idea. There is often a lot hidden in the small print, and a lawyer can check if there is anything glaring that you need to know about.

Remember, you might not need all these agreements as part of your business; hell, you might not need any! But if you do, it's a good idea to talk to your lawyer and get their advice on the contract before it's signed on all sides. It might seem like another step to take and another task to complete before you can launch your business, but it might prevent a nightmare from coming true further down the line.

It's not a step worth missing!

***

Business Insurance

Every business will need a specific type of insurance according to the goods and services they provide. This will be different for every business, so yet again, you need to do some research and find out the exact type of insurance you need to get the right coverage.

Protecting your business against adverse issues, such as financial loss as a result of property damage, lawsuits, theft, illnesses or injuries to your employees, and loss of income for whatever reason, is vital.

Flying solo without insurance is an extremely risky business. Sure, flying by the seat of your pants is good sometimes, but not in this case. You've worked hard to build your business, and you don't want some random occurrence to tear it down. The right insurance coverage will give you protection and peace of mind.

Time to go shopping! There are different premiums, levels of coverage, and plenty of small print you need to make sure you understand. Never sign an insurance contract without completely knowing what you're getting into, it might mean having a knowledgeable friend help you out.

There can be many hidden clauses in insurance contracts that you won't have the first clue about unless you're patient enough to read through that tiny writing in the terms and conditions. I know, who has time for that, right? Well, you're going to have to have time. Common issues are being unable to make a claim within the first few months or a year or similar problems that could land you in hot water if you think you're covered, and it turns out you're not.

Just be aware before you sign on the dotted line, and you'll find a policy that's right for you in all cases.

It's also worth mentioning that there are different types of insurance for different situations. As we mentioned with the contracts earlier, you might not need all types of insurance, but the difference here is that you will definitely need some. A few common types of insurance you may need include:

- **General liability insurance** - Protects your business against claims related to property damage (caused by what your business does) or bodily injury.
- **Professional liability insurance** - Also known as errors and omissions insurance, it protects your business if you receive a claim related to inadequate work or negligence.
- **Property insurance** - A must if you have a brick-and-mortar shop. This type of insurance protects your building and physical assets against damage, theft, or destruction, e.g., from adverse weather conditions.
- **Business interruption insurance** - Be sure to read the small print if you take out this type of insurance because several events aren't covered, but for those that are, this insurance will protect you against loss of income.
- **Commercial auto insurance** - If you have vehicles you use to carry out your business, e.g., a delivery van, then this insurance covers any repairs or replacement costs.

- **Workers compensation insurance** - If any of your employees are injured at work, this type of insurance will cover claims for medical expenses and any loss of earnings.
- **Cyber liability insurance** - This is a must these days. With so much of the world online, it's essential to be protected against online threats; the online world isn't a friendly place! Therefore, cyber liability insurance protects you against cyber attacks, data breaches, and cyber-related events and issues.

***

Knowing How to Pay Your Taxes

Once you've got a business tax number, you can register your business with the tax people and find out how you pay your taxes each year. Again, this varies wildly from country to country, so it comes down to research.

If you're in the US, you'll register to pay taxes with the IRS. If you're in the UK, you'll pay HMRC, and the list goes on.

For most businesses, you'll pay your tax at the end of the financial year, and you'll need to have in-depth figures ready to file your taxes and find out the damage you'll need to cover. That's why proper accounting is so important; it's not only legally required, but it will make your life so much easier when tax time comes.

Of course, you won't pay tax straight away, and you might wonder why you need to think about this right now, but it's the foundations of your business that you need to cover. You also need to register for tax as soon as you start your business so that the appropriate tax departments know you exist.

If you're based in the US, corporations are usually required to pay owed tax on income every year. There is a deadline for filing your corporate taxes and paying whatever you owe by 15 April of the following. So basically, you're always a year behind when you're paying your taxes. That's why it's so vital to stay on top of things; it's very easy to forget what happened a year ago.

Most countries have a revenue threshold you need to reach before you pay any tax. In the US, the minimum revenue before you have to pay tax is $25,000 in a tax year. But remember, this varies from country to country, so don't rely upon the numbers and rules from one country being the same or even similar to another.

In the end, tax issues are one of the trickiest parts of starting a business, but as long as you get all the information you need and tick the necessary boxes, you won't have any nasty surprises to deal with further down the line. It's a headache, for sure, but it's one you'll have to deal with, unfortunately.

However, you can make everything easier by working alongside your accountant. They can help you register everything and keep you on track. This is particularly useful if you're not great with numbers, and it also means that you won't have to remember dates when taxes have to be in - your accountant will remind you ahead of time.

***

Keeping up With Changing Needs

Okay, so now you know the general things you need to cover to start a business and get all the red tape out of the way. But I'm sorry to say that things change occasionally! So, you need to keep updated with new developments and changing needs.

The good news is that if anything like this changes, it will be big news, and you'll hear about it as a business owner. You'll see it on the news, get a letter about it, or hear about it from other business owner friends and connections. It won't be information you have to dig for, but it doesn't hurt to do a quick search every now and then to make sure.

Just don't assume that nothing ever changes when it comes to business guidelines and laws. Government policies constantly change, sometimes affecting what you need to do as an owner. By keeping up to date with everything, you'll cover what you need to cover without any unnecessary sweating.

For instance, the rate of tax can sometimes change. While you won't have to do anything other than just pay what they ask of you, it's important to know so you can budget accordingly. It never hurts to keep ahead of the game, and as a business owner, that's something you need to get used to doing if you want to be super-successful.

And you want to be successful, right?

***

Ready For Some Homework?

There's a lot of information to digest here. It's tempting to rush because it's not all that interesting, and taxes are always yawn-some, but just bribe yourself with something nice to get it done properly. That way, you'll find your business runs much smoother and with less stress.

So, what's your homework for this chapter?

- Write a list of all the elements covered in this chapter, with space to write under each one
- Research what you need to do for every one of them and write it underneath each appropriate heading
- Choose one thing to work on every few days. Don't try to do it all at once. Otherwise, you'll confuse yourself. When you've completed that, move on to the next.
- When you've done them all, have a big glass of wine!

Chapter Nine

All the Pretty Things: Branding & Advertising

Okay, so you can take a breath. The initial financial stuff and all that irritating red tape is done. Pat yourself on the back. You've come a long way!

From this point on, the exciting stuff gets underway. You're starting a business! By now, it should feel like a reality; you're about to become a business owner, and the sky's the limit.

So, what's the next thing? Branding and advertising.

See that sounds much lighter than the heavy details we've talked about so far, doesn't it?

But that doesn't mean you shouldn't pay less attention to this part of the game. Branding is super-important. How you brand your products and services could make or break your business. Remember, people like pretty things. How many times in the past have you been attracted to a product because of how it looks?

Maybe you didn't even need it, but it looks so shiny and cute that you just had to have it. It's a common situation and one you can take advantage of by choosing the right type of branding and marketing strategy.

Now, this part of the journey might not be a huge deal for you. It depends on what your business is. Some businesses might not need an online presence or social media platform, while others will rely heavily on it.

But from now on, if you're a creative person, you will get excited with this part!

***

Branding? What's That All About?

When you were younger, did your parents ever tell you that you "eat with your mouth, not your eyes?" Most kids look at food and decide whether they want to eat it or not in just a second or two, based entirely on its appearance. That kind of mindset is exactly how customers are going to decide whether or not to buy your products or services.

Put simply, we buy with our eyes first.

Branding covers different things: It's your company's logo, the color palette you use to market your products, the font you use, any taglines you want to use pertinent to your business, and the packaging of your products and services, if necessary.

Let's choose an obvious example here and look at the power of branding. Let's go with Mcdonald's.

Everyone knows Maccy D's or whatever you call it in your part of the world. Not only is it a hugely successful company, but it's got unique and strong branding. That's part of why we know what it is without thinking too much about it. The same goes for Coca-Cola and even Apple.

All these companies have a specific design for their logo and any marketing material they use. Apple has that gray, sleek, and minimalist look to everything they put out. Mcdonald's has the famous 'M' arches, with red and yellow across every item they put out. Coca-Cola has that red and white design that fits with everything they do.

While you're not going to reach the industry highs of Mcdonald's anytime soon (let's be realistic here), that doesn't mean you can't prepare for your future success. Strong branding helps people to understand who you are without having to speak. They can recognize you anywhere you go, and if you ensure that everything you put out is high quality, they'll remember that quality when they see your logo or hear your tagline. After all, everyone thinks of Mcdonald's when they hear "I'm lovin' it."

It's time to put on your creative thinking cap and ponder these questions:

- What colors spring to mind when you think of your business? Scribble down whatever comes to you without overthinking.
- What kind of font fits best? Is it something fun and bold? Or perhaps something serious and traditional?

Do you see swirly writing, or do you see something more handwriting-like? Again, don't overthink this. Just brainstorm for now.

- Are there any images that fit with your logo? For instance, Apple has the half-eaten apple logo. Is there anything that immediately jumps into your mind?

If you're unsure about the color scheme or have some clues but are struggling to decide, you could research color psychology.

This is a theory that different colors affect our moods. Color psychology is often used in marketing because the idea is that by making your prospective customers feel a certain thing, you can persuade them to buy your product without even having to do very much.

- **Blue** - Trust, security, power, confidence, purpose, success
- **Purple** - Imagination, justice, spirituality, fantasy, art, mystery, royalty
- **Pink** - Femininity, intuition, calm, softness, gratitude, respect, creativity
- **Red** - Excitement, adventure, strength, energy, action, passion
- **Orange** - Enthusiasm, originality, optimism, freedom, pleasure, youth
- **Yellow** - Curiosity, warmth, happiness, positivity, clarity, joy
- **Green** - Nature, prosperity, luck, health, safety, harmony,

loyalty

It might be a good option to do some research into which colors suit which business models based on color psychology. While you shouldn't directly copy other businesses in this regard, you can take hints and see if any of those shades fit into your idea of what you want your branding to be. Remember, it has to sum up your business; you can't have a kids' toys business and have a boring, gray logo. Just like you can't have a tech company with a logo that looks childish.

While you don't need to think about your website right now (that comes next), you might need one at some point. So, when considering ideas for branding, bear that in mind. How will it look on screen, and how will the color scheme work when people are browsing your site online?

At this point, you're playing around with ideas, but in the next section, we will move on to creating a strong and solid brand. So, it's a good idea to get feedback now. Talk to your friends and family about your branding ideas and test it out on them.

Listen to everything they say and remember to remain emotionally detached. You'll get some negative feedback, and if you remain a step back, it won't affect you personally. Instead, you'll see the feedback as a way to improve what you have already and tweak it as you move toward finalizing your branding.

You can't please everyone, so don't look for 'across the board' thumbs-up, but see which ideas work best and which receive less than stellar responses.

***

Create a Unique Brand Identity to Stand Out Above the Crowd

If you're still totally clueless about this and your mind is blank when you try to come up with ideas, you can enlist a graphic designer's help. However, if you do that, you need to give them plenty of information about who you are as a business so they can capture that in image form. After all, your branding has to say a lot about who you are. It has to sum up your business in a logo.

If you go with a graphic designer, make sure they give you several options. This is likely to be the case anyway, but ask for a series of ideas to look at and decide if you immediately like any of them or if you like the look of one design but might want a few tweaks.

Or, of course, you can do all of this yourself with a notebook and pencil and do some sketches. The old-fashioned route isn't obsolete yet!

Your logo is a visual representation of your brand and should be instantly recognizable. That means it can't look anything like another company's logo. If it does, they're going to confuse you, which could be a long-term pain. Plus, it doesn't show much originality, does it?

Another thing to remember when putting together your logo is that it needs to be adaptable. People will see your logo everywhere; on the TV, websites, desktop computers, and their mobile devices, so it needs to be scalable so it doesn't look out of whack on different platforms.

Once you have your logo down, you can move on to thinking about a tagline, if you want one, of course. Not all businesses have tag lines; Apple and Microsoft don't, and they're doing just fine! But if something catchy and original comes to mind, use it. A tagline helps to cement your brand in the minds of your customers.

In the UK, there is an optometrist called 'Specsavers.' Their tagline is 'should've gone to Specsavers ...' and it's used in jokes and memes all the time, such as when a famous footballer misses a goal.

Even if someone has never used Specsavers, they still know the company due to its tagline. Then, when they need an optometrist, guess who will be the first company they think of?

Yep, you guessed it!

Your Brand Should Reflect What You're About

It's not just about creating a pretty logo and making sure people know the name of your business. They also need to know what you're about and what is important to you. This is all part of your branding journey.

A unique brand identity is the foundation for a recognizable brand. It should reflect your company's values and mission, and it has to be consistent across all social media channels, websites, and platforms. Once you create an identity, you can't confuse people by changing it every so often!

So, how do you create this identity?

It's about consistency and ensuring that every decision you make regarding marketing and advertising sums up your business and what it stands for. For instance, if you're creating organic cosmetics and part of your mission statement is a commitment to being environmentally friendly, you must show that in your branding. Go with natural colors and a gentle appearance. Make sure that your environmental friendliness is evident in every advert or post you make.

Doing that will create an identity of being a planet-conscious company. People will associate you with that value no matter what new product you put out.

***

Creating Your Brand Story

Another way to stand out is to create your brand's story. This is where you need to tag on the heartstrings or poke at a funny bone. Your story needs to tell people who you are and what's important and reflect your mission. Connect with your customers emotionally by showing that you understand their needs and that you're the one to solve them or provide for them.

How do you do this? It's pretty easy, really:

- **Who are your target audience?** From your market

research, who is your ideal customer? Are they young? Middle-aged? Older? Are they married/single/divorced? Do they care about the environment? Do they have a specific need?

- **Create a brand story that targets your audience.** So, if your audience is young Gen Z'ers who are passionate about saving the planet, your story needs to show those people that you're the same as them and that you care about what they care about. That your business was created to do something about these problems.

- **Keep it short and snappy.** You're not writing a novel here; you need to keep your story down to a paragraph at most. The best starting point is to brainstorm and then write and condense. You might need to do this several times before you get it right, but however you do it, make sure your story is engaging and creates an emotional connection between your business and your ideal customers.

- **Test it out.** Share your story with a select few, such as friends, family, and people who fit into your target audience. See what their feedback is and remember to keep an emotional distance from any negative feedback; remember, people love to be negative for the hell of it. But that doesn't mean you should ignore this feedback. It means you should take it into account only and make the necessary tweaks you feel you need to make.

- **Share your story.** Choose where to share your story carefully. Don't flood every single channel with it; people will get fed up hearing 'your truth.' It seems like everyone needs to share their truth lately! Instead, be strategic.

Your website, social media platforms, and advertising campaigns are the best places to tell your tale.

Your branding needs to be on every item of advertising that you put out, be it on social media or via paper-based media. However, it goes without saying that it also needs to be all over your packaging.

If you need to package your goods to send to customers, you must ensure that your logo and any other branding material look good on your packaging and that it showcases whatever is inside. After all, you need to get people excited to open up the box/bag and enjoy whatever they've purchased!

As before, people like pretty things. I know I do.

Quality Counts!

Taking your time with branding is important. You have to show that you're taking this seriously, and you do that by focusing on quality. It has to be at the forefront of every single one of your branding efforts, from your products, packaging, and customer service.

Always ensure that you deliver the best quality possible in everything you do. Remember that you have competitors; if you slip up, they'll be only too happy to swoop in and steal that customer away from you. You'll then end up kicking yourself because you'll know deep down that you could have done better.

With everything you do, ask if it's the best quality you can provide. If it's not, stop and change it. It's not worth cutting corners or half asking anything; it will come back to bite you, believe me. Word-of-mouth marketing has serious power, and if one customer tells another about how they're disappointed in your service, that word will get around faster than the flu. That's not what you want.

Aside from quality, you also need to make sure that you're being consistent. We touched upon this earlier, but it's vital that once you decide on your branding, you stick with it. Use the same fonts, colors, tagline, and messaging across all platforms. That way, people will recognize your brand instantly.

Remember the Mcdonald's example we gave earlier? Can you imagine if Mcdonald's randomly decided to change their logo because they were bored with it? Everyone would be up in arms. Consistency makes people feel comfortable with you as a brand and feel like they can rely on you, almost as a trusted friend. Remember, people don't like shocks or surprises!

Let People Know About You with Clever Marketing

Once your branding is sorted out, it's time to market your business and get the word out!

Marketing, of course, is the art of promoting your business and the goods and services you provide. How you do that depends on the business you have and what you're delivering in the first place.

For instance, marketing a physical store selling clothes will be very different from marketing an online writing business.

So, you need to target your marketing efforts to your ideal customers. Create a persona for your ideal customer in your mind. What do they like? What do they dislike? How do they spend their days? What catches their attention? When you know the answers to these questions, you can tailor your marketing efforts toward them much more easily. You'll find your results are much better too.

The other question is, where do they hang out? That's where you need to concentrate your marketing. If your ideal customer spends a lot of time looking at cosmetics on Instagram, that's where you need to be. Similarly, these types of groups are on Facebook. All of this loops back to your market research, and you'll find a lot of information in that initial lot of research you did.

But don't always assume that social media is the route you need to go down. For sure, it's super-useful, but if your business doesn't necessarily need it, it's just a waste of time.

Some businesses will thrive on social media marketing, and if that's the case for you, you'll need to have a strong presence on Facebook, Instagram, and Twitter as the basics. But if you think that you can get by without it for now, go for it. You can always sign up later on.

There is no 'one size fits all' route to marketing your products or branding. You need to understand your business idea and your target audience inside out. That way, you'll instinctively know the best moves to make versus the ones that won't bring you much joy.

***

Measuring Your Marketing Efforts

Pretty soon after you launch your business, you'll come to realize that you need to do a lot of measuring. No, I'm not talking about tape measures. You need to measure if what you're doing is working. Don't waste time and money on a campaign if it's not. Tweak your strategy or go a different route, as marketing is often trial and error. Have a firm grasp of your target audience's preferences to cut down on errors.

Before you start marketing, set some measurable goals for your business. That way, you can continue to measure them at specific spots along the way. This will help you measure your success and determine what you could do better versus what you need to do more of.

An example of a goal could be to sell your first 100 units in one month. Or it could be to break even in three months. Regarding marketing, a goal could be to see a set number of conversions on your Google Ads after two months.

These are all simple but fantastic goals that can easily be measured.

Keep an Eye on The Competition

As you're starting to get word of your business out there, don't become distracted and avoid checking in on the competition. What are they doing to promote their services? What does their website tell you, and what can you pull from their social media platforms and posts?

You shouldn't copy what your competitors are doing, but by being aware of their moves, you can make better moves at the same time as, or even better, just before them.

By doing this, you can identify your competitor's strengths and weaknesses. You can figure out what they're doing right and aim to implement that into your strategy and what they're doing wrong. You can use those wrong steps as warning signs of what you should avoid too.

Keeping an eye on your competitors doesn't mean that you're copying them or merging their strategy into yours. It means that you can use that information to differentiate your business and set yourself apart.

Nobody likes a copycat.

A Word About Websites & Social Media

I've mentioned a few times so far about social media and the online world, and to what degree you use these depends on your business. However, at the very least, you should have a website.

An up-to-date, attractive, and information-packed website serves several purposes: it helps you connect with your customers, gives them somewhere to get information, and helps you create an emotional connection. It's beneficial to add personal touches, such as a blog, competitions, and surveys.

Of course, the design of your website has to be in keeping with your brand, as we mentioned earlier. But if all of this sounds overwhelming, you can outsource your website-building needs. Using a free website builder is not the best practice because that means you won't have your own ".com" website address. You want to look professional, don't you?

But if you think you can navigate creating your website, well, go for it! It'll certainly save you some money.

Choosing a Website Name

The first thing you want to do is buy a domain. This is your website's name with a ".com" at the end. The most popular site to buy a domain from is Namecheap. You can enter your desired website name to see if it is available here. Truth be told, your dreams might get shattered to realize your desired name is not available.

Tips for choosing a website name, I hope it is obvious that you would prefer it to be as close as possible to your business name. But maybe your business name is a tiny bit too lengthy. Think of how you can shorten it. Or perhaps you can add a prefix that is suitable to your business and branding. The other thing you can consider is not using a ".com", but maybe if you are in Australia, then you can consider ".au" or for the UK, then use "co.uk".

The thing is ".com" is the most established and recognizable domain extension, so it is the first choice for many businesses. It is also the most easily remembered, as the term ".com" is often associated with websites. It is also the first choice for many search engines when ranking websites, so it can help you rank better in searches. Additionally, many users assume that a website ending in ".com" is a legitimate business, so it can help lend credibility to your website. But this is not the bees knees! Whatever works best for you.

Time to Build Your Website

Once you have a website name that you want you are ready to start building your website. There are a few website builders you can choose from which are relatively easy to use. You do not need to be a fancy website developer and have special coding skills. These days most of these website builders have in-app themes where you can drag and drop and upload your images. But I will suggest that you run over to YourTube or Udemy and crash course yourself.

Let me give you a list of the most popular builder sites to choose from, Wix, Weebly, Squarespace, GoDaddy, WordPress, and the list goes on.

On to Social Media

As for social media, this depends on your business model. Remember that you can reach far more people using social media than word-of-mouth marketing. The problem is that keeping your social media platforms and website up to date can often feel like a full-time job, but again, you can outsource that.

Once again you need to choose your "handle" name. This is your username to identify you on social platforms. You want this to be the same as your business name and website. With the growing population, everyone is online these days, so there might be a chance your desired name is not an option. Brainstorm some ideas on how you can tweak it without losing your brand story, customers need to recognize you across all platforms offline and online.

The online world has major ups and downs, but for new business owners, it's often an invaluable way to get the word out and showcase your brand. So, think carefully to which degree this suits your business right now, and remember that it's something you can add at a later date.

Let's Set Some Homework

You should never rush creating your branding. You can't change this halfway through the first year if you change your mind; you're just going to confuse your customers, and it looks super unprofessional. Therefore, it's important to do your due diligence before making a final decision.

I know it's a huge decision, but it's a fun one, right? At least you're not calculating numbers and dealing with paperwork at this point!

So, what's your homework for this chapter? Well, you have two tasks. First, I want you to create a mood board. You can head over to Pinterest and make a digital one. Or you can grab some scissors and glue and go the old-fashioned route. Either way works.

Use your board to log ideas about what you might like your branding to look like. Choose colors, ideas for fonts, tag lines you come up with, and pictures that help to trigger ideas in your mind.

Secondly, check out these two websites and use them to explore fonts and color palettes, **Coolors & Fontpair**.

At this point, you're not making solid decisions. You're exploring ideas and allowing your imagination to run wild. Do this for a week or two, and once your inspiration has run out, sit down with your mood board and start pulling firm plans together.

Remember to ask for advice from those around you, but always go with your gut. This has to be your vision, not the vision of your neighbor or your great-aunt.

Chapter Ten

All By Myself .... Or Not!

Your launch date is getting ever closer, and things are now starting to fall into place. You'll be feeling two main emotions by this point: total excitement, and probably a bit of fear too. You might start questioning whether you're doing the right thing and whether all this work is worthwhile but remember your 'why!'

It's very normal to second guess something as big as starting a business as the reality starts to dawn. Up until now, you might have half thought it wouldn't happen. Perhaps you considered it something you wanted to come true, but you were scared something would steamroll in and stop you. If you were waiting for that thing to come your way, you might want to stop for a second and question whether this is what you want!

However, for the most part, a little fear is normal. In fact, a little fear is a good thing. It means you care.

There's one more thing you might feel at this point - a little overwhelmed.

There is so much going on, and you're doing your best to maintain a solid home and work-life balance. It's quite natural to feel like there's a lot to do and not enough time. While you might have a launch date in your mind right now, it's okay to put it back a couple of weeks if it's making you feel super stressed out. Don't stress yourself out before you even start!

But there's another thing that can help you feel less stressed and effectively give you more time in your day. Outsourcing.

I've mentioned outsourcing a few times throughout the book already, but I want to really zone in on it in this chapter. The reason is that it's a 50/50 deal. If you find the right person to outsource to, your life will become a lot easier, and you'll be able to focus on the areas where you shine. But if you choose the wrong person, your life will be infinitely harder. For that reason, let's focus on how to find the right person to outsource to, what you can outsource, and how you should manage it all.

You're Not Invincible

You might think you can do it all, you've got a handle on everything, and you don't want anyone else putting a meddling hand into your shiny, new business. That's fine, but remember that you're not invincible. Businesses rarely manage to run completely smoothly with just one person doing everything; there are usually bumps along the way, and you're going to need to reach out for advice at the very least.

Of course, it depends heavily upon what your business is. If you're going to be a freelance graphic designer, you don't need anyone else to help you with your work right now. In the future, if your business grows massively, you might want to employ other graphic designers to help you manage the load, but right now, you're golden.

However, what about the financial and legal side of things? Are you an expert in those areas? Probably not. In that case, you might want to seek the help of an accountant to run the finances so you can focus on the design side of your work.

Even the smallest businesses often reach out for help at some point, maybe not right at the beginning, but as things start to take off, you might find yourself trying to juggle too many balls in the air all at once. The chances of you dropping one are pretty high, right?

One dropped ball can have a domino effect on the rest of your business. If you take your eye off that ball and it goes rolling around on the floor, you'll need to stop doing something else to go and pick it up. Then, that other thing starts to suffer, and so on. Can you see how easy it is for everything to begin unraveling if you try to take too much on yourself?

You're not an island, and although I know you probably want to prove yourself to be this super-successful new business owner, it's probably not the best outlook to have.

Reaching out for help and delegating tasks if you're not an expert is smart business. Don't waste time trying to learn something you're not qualified in; seek a professional and focus on what you're good at.

On the whole, outsourcing is a good choice when the task at hand is quite technical. If it would take you a long time to learn and you still might need to ask questions every step of the way, it's not a good investment of your time. You're better off paying someone else who has all the skills.

So, if you're not sure about something, ask. Reach out to people with the answers and ask the questions you're struggling with. It isn't a weakness! And if you think it's a far more productive use of your time to outsource rather than to learn yourself, go for it. A little later in this chapter, I will talk to you about where to find people to outsource to and what to look for.

Develop a Passion for Learning

It might be that you're dead against outsourcing because you've had a bad experience or don't want to pay someone else at this point in your business journey. Maybe you can consider it in the future, but for now, you might prefer to expand your skill set and learn for yourself.

That's fine too. Remember, there's no right or wrong way here. It's your business!

You're not born knowing how to do everything, so you need to read, ask, and learn. You don't need to go to night school or spend a lot of time reading books; there are plenty of ways to learn online. For instance, you can head to YouTube and learn how to do particular tasks or find a course to follow on Udemy. You don't need to splash the cash to learn the basics of any task.

See your business as a personal development tool as much as your passion and method of growing and making money. You'll learn so much as you move through the years, and you have your new business to thank. So, start to see learning as something that is a huge part of your passion, and you'll be more likely to take on board new knowledge and use it in your day-to-day business operations.

Of course, the other thing is to learn from other people's mistakes. It might sound negative, but if the lessons are there, why not learn from them?

Look at businesses with a similar model to yours and research the mistakes they have made. Identify what those mistakes are and then delve a little deeper into what caused them. For instance, did they throw too much money at marketing too early after their launch and then run out of money before they had time to make a profit?

Maybe they didn't focus enough on customer service and started to lose customers as a result. Whatever it was, try and work out the key contributors to the problem and how you can safeguard against it happening to you.

There are many opportunities to learn out there, and you just need to be open to soak up that knowledge like a business-focused sponge.

***

What Can You Outsource?

You can outsource anything you like, but outsourcing everything is not wise! Remember, whenever you outsource something, you'll need to pay the person doing it. People don't tend to respond well to being asked to do things for free! Obviously, you could ask a friend or family member to do something for you, but you'll probably want to reimburse them for their time in some way.

However, if you're going to outsource, the point is that you should give the responsibility for the task to someone with the skills and knowledge to do it and do it well. That means a professional.

Some of the most common tasks that new businesses outsource are:

- **Accounting/book-keeping** - While you can use accounting software and it does a huge amount of the work for you, there's still a lot of knowledge required to keep records correctly and to file your taxes at the right time. Outsourcing this task means you don't need to worry about it all, which is a huge weight off the mind.

- **Graphic design** - At the branding point and when you're developing your packaging, hiring a graphic designer can be the difference between a high-quality logo and setup and one that looks a little amateur. Remember, people judge on how your products and brand is presented to the world; we're visual creatures.

- **Website design** - Setting up a website is possible for even a novice, but if you want a high-quality site, you might want to hire a website designer to do the honors. Once it's all set up, you can easily manage the running of it by keeping it up to date and ensuring the site is running as it should.

- **Online content/SEO** - If you have a blog or any written content on your website or social media, then you might like to outsource it to a freelance writer with SEO knowledge (search engine optimization). Their job is to create and optimize the content with keywords and other strategies to help it reach as high up on the first page of Google search results as possible. That's how you get noticed.

- **Social media management** - If your business is going to need a heavy social media presence, then you're going to find managing all platforms pretty time-consuming. It will no doubt take your time and attention away from everyday operations, so hiring someone to do this for you could be a huge relief.

- **Marketing** - Some businesses outsource their marketing needs to someone experienced in this field who can create a strategy and monitor its success. Whether you choose to do this depends on how much time you have and how confident you are to do it yourself.

Ultimately, you can outsource whatever you see fit, but remember that you're never going to learn if you outsource everything.

If there's one thing you shouldn't outsource, it's your customer service. Some people do this, but you need to know that any complaints or problems are handled in the way you would want them to be handled. Remember, people will judge your business based on quality and how you treat people. If you outsource something as critical as this, your customers may not get the right level of service. It depends on who you outsource it to, of course, but you know your business, and you have its values and beliefs at the heart of everything; after all, it came from you.

When problems arise, especially at the start, you need to make sure that they're handled carefully and personally. You may find that if you outsource this key element, you lose control over how things are handled, and it may spiral into something you aren't happy with.

***

Where to Find Someone to Outsource

Once you've decided what you will outsource, the next logical question is where to find someone to do the job. This is where it might get tricky.

You need to feel in your bones that you've chosen the right person. They need to understand your business and what it's about; it's no good choosing someone who is happy to do a job at half the effort level and just take the money. You won't get the quality service you deserve; in that case, you might as well just do it yourself.

I don't want to be negative here and make you feel like finding the right person is difficult. There are some fantastic freelancers out there. You just need to find the right one for you. You can do that by knowing what you need and want in a person who works for you and then by taking your time when hiring them. Don't rush!

The best places to find people to outsource to are online. Check out freelancing websites, such as Upwork or Fiverr. A few other notable sites include Freelancer, PeoplePerHour, Guru, and Outsource Accelerator. You can also check out LinkedIn and social media groups related to the niche you're looking to outsource.

On freelancing sites, you'll sign up as a client and post a job. Then, you'll wait for people to apply for the job. You'll shortlist and interview them before choosing the person to go with. On other sites, like LinkedIn and social media, it's about looking for people who seem to be experts in their niche and then approaching them directly to discuss further.

***

What to Look for When Outsourcing (& What to Avoid)

When you find the right person you click with, they will become an integral part of your business and take a massive weight off your shoulders. In the journey to finding that person, there are a few things that fall into the do and don't category.

Let's look at those in this section, so you can find the perfect person to help you out rather than cause you a migraine.

Things to look out for in a freelancer/someone to outsource to:

- **Experience/reviews** - Find out details about this person's experience and exactly what they've done in the past. How long have they been working in this niche? Who have they worked for before? Do they have references you can check? Taking whatever someone says at face value is not always a good idea, so references and reviews are an excellent way to determine if a person is as good as they say they are.

- **Qualifications** - This may not be something you need to look for, but if you're outsourcing your accounting work, you'll need a qualified accountant. Don't opt for someone who just says they're good with numbers; anyone can use a calculator.

- **Happy to meet via video call** - Some people don't want to go through the selection process when applying for a job in this way; they prefer to apply and then get to work. But it's a good idea to meet up with this person over video call and see if you vibe with them personally. Remember, it's not all about the quality of the job they can do for you but how you connect with them too.

- **Transparency** - While you should never micromanage someone you outsource to, you should be able to contact them and check in with them from time to time. After all, they're working for you. This means they should be transparent in everything they do, and they're okay with you checking in for a quick update sometimes. But of course, don't go over the top with this; otherwise, you'll just scare them away!

- **Easy to contact** - Moving on from the last point, you need someone who is contactable at roughly the same time as you, so if you're going to hire someone from a different time zone, make sure they're contactable at specific times of the day.

Things to avoid:

- **Zero experience** - While everyone has to start somewhere, that doesn't mean you should give chances to people with no experience to show. Yes, you'll be able to pay them less, but is it worth it if you risk the quality of work done? Maybe you'll find someone new on the block who's amazing, but the chances of that are quite slim.

- **Someone who is very rigid in their work processes** - While you should never go in there and dictate exactly how you want them to work, you should look to avoid people who are very rigid and refuse to compromise. Remember, they're the ones with the skills, so you should allow them to lead on this, but if you have a specific request or requirement and they seem pretty keen to avoid it, it's a red flag. It simply means that you won't get along well and will always be battling to get things done in a way that reflects your business values.

- **Opposing time zones** - This doesn't mean you should never employ someone from another country or even continent. But having wildly different time zones isn't going to work. For instance, if you're in the UK and they're in Australia, you will always miss one another! Make sure that they're willing to work during the times when you can get in touch.

- **Unprofessional types** - This is a no-brainer, but I have to mention it. You might mistake their unprofessional nature for someone who's easygoing. There's a big difference between being easygoing and easy to work with and being unprofessional and cutting corners. You'll usually get a sense of this when you meet them on a video call, but also from their reviews.

- **Poor reviews** - This leads me to this next point! See what I did there? Basically, it's a good idea to avoid anyone with a series of poor reviews. If there's only one, give them the benefit of the doubt; some people have nothing good to say. But if you see many bad reviews, it's a good reflection of the fact that they're not the right choice for you or anyone else.

You should treat finding a freelancer or person to outsource to the same as you would finding a regular employee. It's basically the same thing, but the chances of meeting in real life are slim! It's as much about personality as skills and qualifications in many ways; this person has to fit in with your business values and ethos. If they don't, they'll cause you problems without even meaning to.

Of course, you might only employ them to do one quick job for you, which is the end of the contract. If they do a good job, stay in touch with them and reach out to them in the future if you have any similar tasks. This can be part of your networking, and it's always good to have someone reliable to contact if the need arises.

Once you think you've found the right person, how do you get your arrangement started? There are many things you need to keep in mind here. But once you iron out these issues, you can look forward to a harmonious working relationship with someone who can do a great job for you on a task you can't do yourself or simply don't want to.

***

How to pay

You may or may not choose to have a vendor or employment contract with this person. It depends on how much they will help you and how often. If they're just going to sort out your branding and then the job is done, you won't need this. You could ask them to sign a non-disclosure agreement (more on that shortly), but other than that, it will be a freelancer arrangement done via a freelancing website, in all likelihood.

Work out between you how much you will pay this person for the work they're going to do. If they're going to do a continuous task for you, e.g., your accounts, then you'll need to agree to a monthly salary/retainer.

If they're going to do one task for you, are you going to pay them per hour? In that case, you'll need them to give you an honest estimate of how long the job will take. Or are you going to pay them a fixed amount for the task?

Head online and research average rates for this type of task and then negotiate to come to a fair price for both of you. Don't try to sell this person short; at the end of the day, they're trying to make a living like you, and if you want quality, you'll have to pay for it.

Consider a non-disclosure agreement

I've just mentioned this, and it's something you should definitely consider. A non-disclosure agreement means that this person isn't allowed to disclose any information about your business to anyone else. It covers the work they've done and any company information they were privy to during the time they worked for you.

As a new business, using this type of agreement is a good idea because it protects you against leaks. You don't want your new competitors to find out your marketing strategy ahead of time. They might not see you as a major threat yet, but they'll know that you're an up-and-coming potential competitor for them, and they'll want to get all the intel on you while they still can. A non-disclosure agreement protects you against such things and is quick and easy to arrange.

You can find standard non-disclosure agreement templates online. Simply personalize it to your needs, and then you sign it, along with the freelancer. They keep a copy, and so do you. If anything was to occur later down the line and you suspect it has something to do with the person who carried out this task for you, you can legally do something about it.

Set out your expectations at the start

I mentioned before that there are a million and one wonderful people out there to take this task off your hands, but there are a few unscrupulous types who will do a fair job or a terrible job, depending on their level of effort. To make sure that you're getting the good ones, set out your expectations for this job from the very start. Don't be afraid to be specific; if they're a good person for you to choose, they'll expect this and probably have a few points of their own to put forward.

So, if you need them to be contactable between specific hours of the day, point that out. If this person cannot do that, either negotiate some middle ground or move on to someone else. If you want to have a video call meeting with them every Friday afternoon, inform them of this and make it a part of your arrangement.

Everything is ten times easier when both sides set out what they want and need from the beginning. Remember, you're probably going to be communicating online or over the phone, and it's super easy for misunderstandings to occur between two people who don't know each other all that well.

Set deadlines for delivery

Finally, whatever task you're outsourcing, set a reasonable deadline for the work to be completed. Be realistic! Give the person enough time to do their thing and work their magic, but make sure that you negotiate a deadline that works for you too.

If they miss the deadline or don't deliver the quality you expect, don't be afraid to contact them and lay out your concerns. Obviously, be polite. Maybe life just got in the way, and something happened. Giving them a chance to explain will keep your positive working relationship ticking along nicely, and get your work done very soon. But if they regularly miss deadlines and don't deliver the work you expect, then you are within your rights to question what's going on, and in the worst cases, terminate the agreement and find someone who can do what they've said they're going to do.

***

Is Outsourcing a Risk?

Look, I'm not going to sugarcoat it. If you find a great person to outsource a task to, they'll make everything easier, and you'll be glad you did it. But if you find someone who doesn't live up to your expectations, it won't be a great experience.

So yes, in some ways, it's a risk.

But is it a risk worth taking?

Remember, your business is your baby, and you will want to protect it at all costs. But that shouldn't mean holding onto it so tight that you refuse to let anyone help you. A quality entrepreneur knows when to stick and when to twist. You'll learn this skill over time, but trust your gut on it; if you feel it's best to delegate this task, go for it.

***

Homework Time!

You might not want to outsource any of your tasks. It might be that you don't need to. If that's the case, carry on as you were and skip this homework task. But if you feel like there is at least one task that another person could help you with, even if just in the short-term, this task will help you.

Grab a piece of paper and write down every task you need to complete from start to finish. Don't miss anything or lump things together to shorten your list! Then, put a star next to the things you can do yourself. Don't take on too much: make sure you only start what you're good at, can do, or don't want to pass on to anyone else.

For the tasks that don't have stars next to them, transfer them to another sheet of paper.

- Which of these tasks can you realistically learn about and do yourself?
- Which of these tasks do you need someone else with more experience to complete?

Now you have a list of the tasks you want to outsource. You can work out your expectations and available budget. Peruse some freelancing sites and find out the going rate for these types of jobs. Once you know the real picture for passing this task over, you can work out whether it’s realistic or whether you really need to get your brain working and learn for yourself!

Chapter Eleven

Ready, Set, Launch!

Everything is in place. You're ready to board the plane and fly into the skies of entrepreneurship for the first time!

You've come so far. Before jumping into launch mode, pat yourself on the back for a second. The planning stages of starting a business are long-winded, but you've made it through and deserve credit. Not everyone gets this far; many people give up when things get a little tough and decide to go back to watching Netflix instead.

Do you feel ready? The hope is that you do. However, it's normal to have a few butterflies at this stage. If you feel like you need more time, hold off a little longer. That doesn't mean procrastinating. It means double-checking that all the i's are dotted, and the t's are crossed.

You're probably realized by this point that a lot of starting a business comes down to planning, and you're not quite done yet! Create a plan with tasks and timelines to avoid missing something important. Then, on the launch date, you can push aside those feelings of "I'm sure I've forgotten something."

But before you press ‘go,’ let’s run through this; and give you a printable guide to work with.

***

What is a Project Plan?

In the business world, there is such a thing as a project plan. It is the list of all your tasks with relative deadlines. Some tasks can run in parallel, but most are critical paths meaning you first have to finish the one before you can start the next one.

If you set some goals with deadlines, you will keep yourself accountable. We all know deadlines are there to be moved. Life happens, and that is okay. But at least you will see that you are making traction as you tick off some of these tasks.

Here is an example of a Project Plan for Starting a Business

Tasks & Subtasks	Your time to complete	Start Date	The moving Deadline
1. Research Mode			
Competitors	2 weeks	01-Feb	15-Feb
Demand	2 weeks	15-Feb	01-Mar
Opportunity	2 weeks	01-Mar	15-Mar
2. All the Numbers			
Break-Even	2 weeks	15-Mar	29-Mar
5-Year Projection	2 weeks	29-Mar	12-Apr
3. The Big Business Plan			
Business Plan	4 weeks	12-Apr	10-May
4. Money, Money, Money			
Finding Capital	4 weeks	10-May	07-Jun
5. Accounting & Legal			
Bank Account	4 weeks	07-Jun	05-Jul
Business License	4 weeks	05-Jul	02-Aug
Tax ID Number	4 weeks	02-Aug	30-Aug
Legal Documents	4 weeks	30-Aug	27-Sep
6. Branding & Marketing			
Website	6 weeks	27-Sep	08-Nov
Marketing Plan	2 weeks	08-Nov	22-Nov

The Importance of Accountability

So many people tell you that you shouldn't plan life out and that you should just fly by the seat of your pants. Well, that might work in some situations, but it's not going to fly here. If you want your business to succeed, you need to lay the groundwork, which means going through every one of the phases in this book.

Each phase is vital to the journey; if you miss one, you won't get off the ground.

So no, planning isn't boring or being far too organized. In the entrepreneurship world, you can never be too organized. Do you think Richard Branson wakes up in the morning and thinks, "Nah, I can't be bothered," so he rolls back over and goes to sleep? Well, maybe, but it's highly unlikely!

Do you think Oprah is so careless that she doesn't think before she acts? Of course, she does! This is a highly successful and measured woman! She knows the importance of planning and is not afraid to do it.

So, you can be a sleeping Richard or a real Richard. You can be a super-organized Oprah or someone who wants to start a business but can't be bothered to go through all the stages properly.

Which is it going to be?

Having a plan means that you can measure your success and progress along the way. Set yourself goals and hold yourself accountable to them. If you've told friends and family members that you're starting a business, you'll hold yourself accountable to them too. You won't want to tell them you gave up and couldn't spare the time, are you?

Keep a visualized picture in your mind of the moment your business hits break even and starts making a profit. Imagine how that feels. Picture the huge smile on your face and that sensation of feeling like everything was worth it because it will be worth it in the end. All of this planning and reading will be worth it, and more.

***

No Homework Today!

I'm not going to give you any homework today! Yes, you've done enough, and you're finally at the point where you can launch your business. So, I figure you've got enough on your plate.

However, if you are studious and you want to keep going, you can write out your to-do list of every task you need to do from start to finish. It might help to focus your mind and show you how much work you have to do. Otherwise, it might seem so overwhelming that you forget where to start.

However, if you don't feel you need a list, simply read through each chapter and work through the homework exercises as you go.

Anyway, you're probably so excited that you won't be able to concentrate on homework!

Conclusion

You've made it! You've reached the end of the book and you now know everything you need to know about starting a business. It's an achievement that you reached this point because it means you're truly serious about what you're about to do.

Pat yourself on the back. Have a glass of wine. Do whatever you normally do when you want to celebrate something.

The truth is that many people have the desire to start a business, but they get sidetracked or decide that it's too much hard work. At some point along the way, they just give up. But you're different, right? You've read this book all the way to the end, even through the numbers and red tape parts, so that means you're dedicated.

That's a great starting point.

Some parts of the process may seem a little overwhelming, and it's likely that some steps just aren't your strong point. That's fine. Nobody is born knowing everything in the world. But you can learn and have everything you need to do that.

If starting a business was as easy as just opening a bank account and setting up a Facebook page, everyone would have been doing it years ago. It's a lot more complicated than that, but breaking each step down into milestones means you'll work through the process without having a major panic at every step.

It's not supposed to be the stressful and terrifying journey many people make it out to be. You're birthing your business here. It's a fun thing! Covering all bases means you care, and that's great preparation for what's to come.

***

When Fear Creeps in, Remember Your Passion

If you do feel overwhelmed at any point, remember your passion. It will be your guiding light whenever you feel a little lost, or it's suddenly gone dark. Sit down, breathe, close your eyes, and focus on your passion. After a while, you'll notice that the " I can't do it" attitude will ebb away, and "I can do it" will replace it.

Because you can do it. You know you can. You just need to go through the process, take your time, and find your way out to the other side.

Of course, starting a business is also about knowing that you might not get it all right the first time. It just means that you need to stop and take a moment to figure things out again. It's easy to take a wrong turn, but that's what maps and GPS were invented for! You can always find your way back again.

If you can adapt quickly and retain that slight separation between you and your business, you'll find it much easier to think, "Hey, this route isn't working. Let's turn back and try another." It won't pull you apart; you'll adapt and change.

Fear is nothing but an illusion. It's a voice in your head that tells you something is too hard or that you just can't do it. Push it aside and stay focused on what you want to do. You haven't read this entire book and got this far just to give up now!

***

You Are Not an Island (How Boring Would That Be?)

The other thing to remember, and something I've mentioned a few times throughout the book, is asking for help. Seriously, don't be too proud. If you want to go around pretending that you know everything and you've got it all covered, you're going to find yourself in a very large hole. One you probably can't dig your way out of.

If you want to know something, ask. If you haven't got a clue where to start, find someone who knows and ask them. You'll learn so much more if you put your pride aside and ask for help.

Remember about outsourcing too. Sometimes it's just the better way forward. It's not about taking the easy way out. It's about managing your time more effectively. If you don't know something, you haven't got the time (or inclination) to learn, and you know someone who is an expert in that area, why not ask them to do it? It makes sense!

The point is that you will need to be open to input from other people if you want this to work. That doesn't mean allowing others to steamroll in and take over; it doesn't mean allowing negative feedback to push you off course. It means being selective but clever with the feedback you allow to influence your decisions.

Remember to stay one step ahead of the game; don't become too emotionally attached to your business idea. I know it's hard, this is your metaphorical baby, and you can't help but want to see it succeed, but if you pour all of yourself into it, you'll suffer in some way or another. Trust me. It's not worth losing friends or a partner over this. Yes, it means a lot to you, but if it's meant to work out, you'll be able to do it without throwing every single hour God sends at it.

So, remember that you are not an island. You need people around you because life would be pretty boring otherwise. Allow those people to help you, but don't allow the Negative Nancies to steamroll in and take over either.

Remember The Six P's

Finally, I want to introduce you to the six P's. They are:

Proper Planning Prevents P!ss Poor Performance

Remember this at all times, especially when you're tired of planning everything out on paper and you just want to get out there and do something practical!

Careful planning will stop you from doing irrational things because you're desperate to just do *something. Anything*. It will make you stop and wait for a second. You need that kind of rationality if you want this to work.

Now, if planning isn't your passion and you find the whole thing to be nothing more than a major mental block, then go ahead and outsource the planning too. You can have a hand in it and approve decisions; someone else can do the leg work. If that's how you want to start your business, that's perfectly fine.

But if you want to have a hand in every step of the way, planning will help you do that.

***

Are You Ready for The Next Step?

I'm about to bid you goodbye and watch you walk off into the sunset, ready to start your new business and take on the world.

I'm proud!

You've come a long way already, and even though there's a good way to go yet, you have all the tools you need to get your job done. If you have nothing but your passion, you're still in a better position than you were yesterday.

So, are you ready to take that next step? If you doubt yourself, remember your 'why' and your passion. If you're unsure of something, ask for help. And if you need a quick reminder of something you need to do, check back on our flight plan chapter, and you'll find what you're looking for.

For now, it's time to say goodbye. I hope reading this book has given you a big push toward finally making your business-owning dream a reality. You really can do it, you know. If not you, then who else?

Good luck. And if you become a millionaire, remember who taught you the basics!

Appendix: Websites Mentioned

Chapter 3 - *Online Reselling*

- eBay - ebay.com
- Poshmark - poshmark.com

Chapter 8 - *Accounting Software*

- QuickBooks - quickbooks.intuit.com
- Sage Business Cloud - sage.com
- Xero - xero.com
- GnuCash - gnucash.org
- Odoo - odoo.com

Chapter 9 - *Let's Set Some Homework*

- Coolors - coolors.co
- Fontpair - fontpair.co

Chapter 9 - *A Word About Websites & Social Media*

- Namecheap - namecheap.com
- Wix - wix.com
- Weebly - weebly.com
- Squarespace - squarespace.com
- GoDaddy - godaddy.com
- WordPress - wordpress.com

Chapter 10 - *Develop a Passion For Learning*

- Udemy - udemy.com

Chapter 10 - *Where to Find Someone to Outsource To*

- Upwork - upwork.com
- Fiverr - fiverr.com
- Freelancer - freelancer.com
- PeoplePerHour- peopleperhour.com
- Guru - guru.com
- Outsource Accelerator - outsourceaccelerator.com
- LinkedIn - linkedin.com

About the Author

Check out Julian's author profile on Amazon.

References

Canada Revenue Agency. (2023, April 4). *Taxes*. Canada.ca. https://www.canada.ca/en/services/taxes.html

HM Revenue & Customs. (2023, March 23). GOV.UK. https://www.gov.uk/government/organisations/hm-revenue-customs

Home | Internal Revenue Service. (n.d.). https://www.irs.gov/

Office, A. T. (2019, February 5). *Home page*. https://www.ato.gov.au/

W. (2023, April 4). *SARS Home | South African Revenue Service*. South African Revenue Service. https://www.sars.gov.za/

What is VAT? (n.d.). Taxation and Customs Union. https://taxation-customs.ec.europa.eu/what-vat_en

Printed in Great Britain
by Amazon

24883106R00109